Name _____

Fold & Read: Nonfiction Checklist

Each time you finish a booklet activity, check or color the matching number space.

1	2	3	4	5	6
7	8	9	10	11	12
13	14	15	16	17	18
19	20	21	22	23	24
25	26	27	28	29	30
31	32	33	34	35	36

Fold & Read: Nonfiction • ©The Mailbox® Books • TEC61375

Table of Contents Booklet

A Blue Frog?

Who's King Tut?

Y0-CCD-249

Answer keys are at the end of the book.

(Cut your answer key pages in half to make cards.)

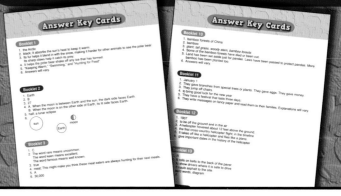

Note to the teacher: If desired, make student copies of the checklist found on the back of the table of contents booklet. Ask each student to keep track of the booklet activities she's completed on her copy.

The MAILBOX®

grades **4–6**

Fold & READ NONFICTION

36 ready-to-fold reading practice booklets

✔ Features engaging informational text

✔ Reinforces core comprehension skills

✔ Builds vocabulary

✔ Develops high-level thinking

✔ Encourages reading strategies

Venus Flytrap

Mystery of the Mastodon

Managing Editor: Becky S. Andrews

Editorial Team: Diane Badden, Kimberley Bruck, Karen A. Brudnak, Pam Crane, Chris Curry, David Drews, Karen Grossman, Tazmen Hansen, Marsha Heim, Lori Z. Henry, Mark Rainey, Greg D. Rieves, Hope Rodgers-Medina, Rebecca Saunders, Todd Savelle, Donna K. Teal, Sharon M. Tresino, Zane Williard

www.themailbox.com

©2013 The Mailbox® Books
All rights reserved.
ISBN 978-1-61276-255-5

Printed in China
10 9 8 7 6 5 4 3 2 1

90323503RRDSZ122012

What's Inside

Already laminated! Simply tear out, fold, and use!

Follow-up questions

Hey! Why Not Write About It?

Dogs communicate in a variety of ways with each other, humans, and other animals. Most pets—whether they are cats, dogs, hamsters, or fish—each have their own way of trying to talk to us at one time or another. Think of your own favorite pet or animal. Write an imaginary conversation with that pet or animal about how your day has been so far.

Booklet 16

Fold & Read: Nonfiction • ©The Mailbox® Books • TEC61376

Write your answers on your paper.

1. Describe what a dog does to indicate that it wants to play.

2. What does the word *primary* mean in the second sentence of the second paragraph?

3. True or false? Barking is a dog's only method for communicating with people.

4. How do you know your answer to number 3 is correct?

5. If your dog is barking, is it a good idea to speak to it in a calm tone? Why or why not?

6. Describe other ways besides barking in which dogs communicate to each other and to humans.

7. Which of the following is the best definition of the word *yelping* in the last paragraph?
   a. to lick
   b. to utter a sharp, shrill cry
   c. to tumble backward
   d. to fall asleep

8. Why is a dog that is scared also a dog that might be dangerous?

Full-color photo

Canine Conversation

Fun-to-read passage

Reading level

Writing connection for early finishers

Readability Code	
◆◆◆◆	= 4.0+
◆◆◆◆◆	= 4.5+
◆◆◆◆◆◆	= 5.0+
◆◆◆◆◆◆◆	= 5.5+

Name _____

Fold & Read: Nonfiction Checklist

Each time you finish a booklet activity, check or color the matching number space.

1	2	3	4	5	6
7	8	9	10	11	12
13	14	15	16	17	18
19	20	21	22	23	24
25	26	27	28	29	30
31	32	33	34	35	36

Table of Contents Booklet

www.themailbox.com/core

Booklet	Title	◆◆◆◆
1	Animal Defenses	
2	The *Whydah*: A Pirate Ship	
3	Just Google It!	
4	Giant Ground Sloth	
5	A League of Their Own	
6	Earth's Natural Satellite	
7	Mighty Mollusks: The Giant Squid	
8	Sequoyah Writes the Cherokee Language	
9	Wild Mustangs	

Answer keys are at the end of the book.
(Cut your answer key pages in half to make cards.)

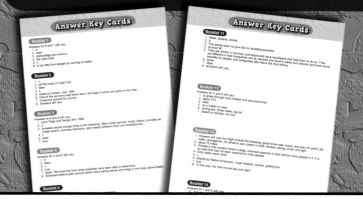

Note to the teacher: If desired, make student copies of the checklist found on the back of the table of contents booklet. Ask each student to keep track of the booklet activities she's completed on her copy.

Hey!
Why Not Write About It?

It's your turn to make up a new animal. Describe where it lives (for example, in a rain forest, a desert, grasslands, an ocean, woodlands). Tell what animal wants to eat it. Finally, tell what type of animal defense it uses to avoid being something's lunch.

Fold & Read: Nonfiction • ©The Mailbox® Books • TEC61376

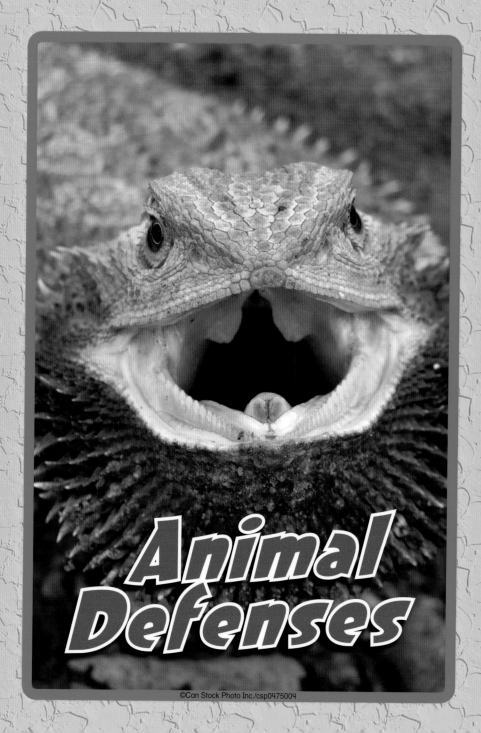

Animal Defenses

Animals use many tricks so they don't end up as breakfast. Some are very good at hiding. Some act like a scary animal. Still others hold very still and look like a leaf or twig. Sometimes an animal uses the special weapons it has. Most animals have some way to avoid the animals that want to eat them.

Camouflage

One way an animal avoids a predator is by blending in. A white-tailed deer is a good example. Its brown color makes it hard to see. The fields and forests where it lives are full of the color brown. You might see this deer only when it is running away. Nature's most famous hide-and-seek animal is the chameleon. Its green skin blends with its forest background. It can also change its color to brown. That way it blends with dead leaves and tree trunks.

Mimicry

The hawk moth caterpillar and the walking stick are two kinds of animals that can pretend to be something else. The hawk moth caterpillar puffs itself up to look like a deadly snake. This can scare away a bird that wants to eat it. The walking stick lives in bushes and trees. This brown and green insect easily looks like a twig or even a leaf. When it stands on a branch and holds still, it is very safe. It's very easy to miss!

Special Defenses

The cane toad lives in the warm and wet parts of Central America, South America, and Australia. It has a weird way of fighting back against animals that want to eat it. The cane toad can squirt poison from glands on its head! The poison can make another animal very sick. For some animals, the cane toad poison is strong enough to kill. And how about the basilisk lizard? It has a very special weapon. It can run on water—away from its enemy!

When it comes to survival in the wild, it makes sense to have some kind of trick that will fool predators. Just ask the cane toad or the walking stick. Animals must be more than just quick to avoid being a bird's breakfast!

Write your answers on your paper.

1. Write the letter of the best meaning for the word *camouflage*, which is the subheading of paragraph 2.
   a. brightly colored clothing
   b. blending in with your surroundings
   c. not moving

2. True or false? The cane toad can run away from danger across the surface of water.

3. What are two ways animals can look like something else in order to avoid being eaten?

4. What animal can squirt poison from its head?

5. Which phrase in paragraph 3 gives the meaning of the word *mimicry*?
   a. can scare
   b. when it stands
   c. to be something else
   d. very easy to miss

6. Which of the three animal defenses described in this passage seems like the best one for an animal to use to avoid being eaten? Why?

7. Of the three animal defenses described in this passage, which one do you think is used the most by animals in the wild? Why?

8. What does a basilisk lizard do to avoid being eaten?

Hey!
Why Not Write About It?

Much of what many of us know about pirates comes from movies. Experts say movie pirates are nothing like the real pirates in the age of sailing ships. Pretend you and your classmates are pirates on a sailing ship. Write about your pirate names and how you got them. Name your pirate ship. Then set sail on a dangerous journey across the ocean. To where are you sailing and why?

Fold & Read: Nonfiction • ©The Mailbox® Books • TEC61376

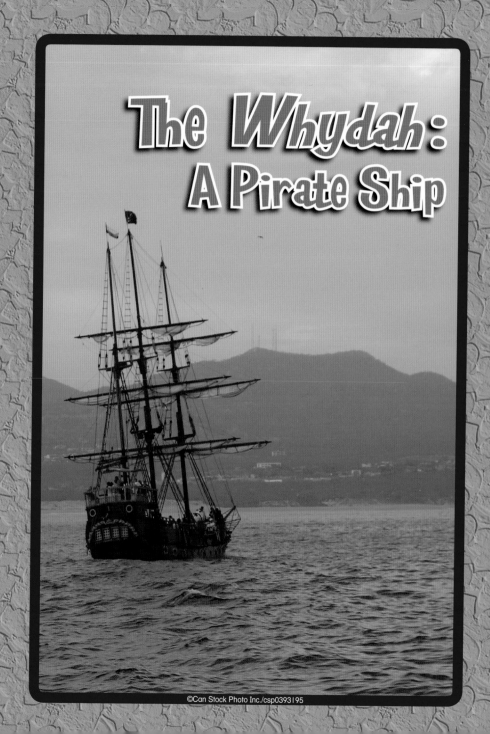

The Whydah: A Pirate Ship

The *Whydah* (WIH-dah) was a sailing ship built in England in 1715. It had three tall masts and was very fast. However, it was not fast enough to sail away from Samuel Bellamy. Bellamy was a famous pirate. He was known as Black Sam because of his dark black hair. In 1717, he chased down the *Whydah* with two pirate ships of his own. Black Sam made the *Whydah* his new pirate ship. He used it to catch still more ships to take their gold, silver, and other treasure.

Soon, Bellamy sailed the *Whydah* up the East Coast. On April 26, 1717, the pirates were off the coast of Cape Cod when they met a fierce storm. Strong winds and rough waves hit the *Whydah*. People on land who saw the storm said the wind blew at over 70 miles per hour. They also said the waves were over 30 feet high. The *Whydah* was doomed.

The waves and wind pushed the *Whydah* into a sandbar. The ship broke apart and sank. Gold, silver, and other riches tumbled into the sea. Only two men lived to tell about the shipwreck. One of them said there were 180 bags of gold and silver on the pirate ship.

For years, people tried to find the *Whydah*'s treasure. No one ever found the bags of silver and gold. At last, treasure hunters found three cannons from the *Whydah* in July, 1984. That's more than 250 years later!

Since 1984, those treasure hunters have found more than 100,000 items from the shipwreck. They have found pirate weapons. They have found dishes, clothes, and shoes. The treasure hunters have even found coins. These objects have been seen at museums around the country. Still, no one has found the bags of silver and gold.

Write your answers on your paper.

1. According to the first paragraph, Sam Bellamy was known as "Black Sam" because
   a. he was always in a bad mood
   b. he dressed in all black clothing
   c. he had dark black hair
   d. he wore a black eye patch

2. Where was Bellamy sailing when the *Whydah* was hit by a violent storm?

3. True or false? The *Whydah* was built in France in 1950.

4. Which one of these things did not cause the *Whydah* shipwreck?
   a. a sandbar   c. strong winds
   b. jagged rocks   d. giant waves

5. Who found three cannons from the wreck of the *Whydah*? When were they first discovered?

6. How do we know there were 180 bags of silver and gold aboard the *Whydah* when it sank?

7. Where can people go to see items brought up from the wreck of the *Whydah*?

8. Do you think there really were 180 bags of gold and silver aboard the ship when it sank? Why or why not?

Hey!
Why Not Write About It?

Imagine that you and a friend are starting a new company. First, think of what your new company would do. Perhaps you'd sell socks with the wearer's name sewn into them. You decide. Then come up with a funny name for your company. How would you make it fun and interesting to work at your new company?

Fold & Read: Nonfiction • ©The Mailbox® Books • TEC61376

Just Google It!

Google. It's a very silly word. It is also a very serious business. The Google search engine is one of the most used on the Internet. Two Stanford University students started Google in 1996. They worked in a garage that a local mom rented to them. Now it is a very big company that does a lot of things. It handles millions and millions of searches each day from all over the world.

Started by Larry Page and Sergey Brin, Google now has more than 30,000 people working all around the globe. Google also offers more than just a search engine these days. It has Gmail email service. It hosts videos at YouTube. You can find pictures of just about anything at Google Images. Plus, it gives you directions to places you want to visit with Google Maps. It also makes software that runs many smartphones.

However, it sure sounds fun to work at a serious company like this one. People who work at Google's main offices can bring their dogs to work. Google offices have couches that look like huge beanbag chairs. There are lava lamps, pianos, game rooms, and more for the people who work there. Free snacks are all over the place.

Google is such a big part of people's lives that the word *google* is now in the dictionary. The word *google* can be used in a sentence such as "Mary needs to google cane toads for her science project." At Google's offices, employees are called *Googlers*. If you are a brand-new Googler, you are called a *Noogler* (a mix of *new* and *Googler*).

This fun company with the silly name is a very serious business!

Write your answers on your paper.

1. Who are the two men who started Google? What year did they start?

2. Which of these definitions fits best in place of *google* in the sentence "Mary needs to google cane toads for her science project"?
   a. use the Internet to research
   b. go to the pet store to purchase
   c. use her smartphone to photograph
   d. none of the above

3. Name three things Google does besides providing a search engine.

4. A *perk* is something other than a paycheck that you get for working at a company. Which of the following is a perk of working at Google?
   a. a free kitten in every office
   b. tickets to the movies every Friday night
   c. free snacks
   d. your own television show on Google TV

5. True or false? Google Images is the name of Google's video-hosting service where you can watch videos online.

6. How do you know your answer for number 5 is correct? Use evidence from the text.

7. True or false? Google makes software to power smartphones.

8. Dogs are welcome in Google's main office. Why do you think cats are not welcome?

Hey!
Why Not Write About It?

Write a short story about your own encounter with the legendary giant ground sloth. Imagine that it takes place in your school yard. Is the sloth friendly? Why does it walk on its hind legs when it is at your school?

Fold & Read: Nonfiction • ©The Mailbox® Books • TEC61376

Giant Ground Sloth

The Amazon rain forest in South America is home to many strange and fascinating creatures. It is also where you will hear stories about a strange, mysterious beast. Scientists say the beast is only a legend. But the people who live in the rain forest say they have seen and heard the monster.

One hunter in the Amazon said, "I was working by the river when I heard a scream." Then he saw what looked like a man coming out of the jungle. He said the shape was covered in hair. It was walking on two legs like a man.

"The moment you hear it, all your hairs stand on end," another hunter explained.

Giant Ground Sloth

People along the Amazon River have described the creature. They say it is covered in long red hair. When it stands on its back legs, it is over six feet tall. Reports say the beast is accompanied by a foul odor. It has huge claws that face backward. They say it is strong enough to tear apart a palm tree so it can eat the tree's soft insides.

One scientist thinks the beast may be a giant ground sloth. Most scientists don't agree. Giant ground sloths became extinct about 10,000 years ago.

But if you stop and think about it, this Amazon rain forest beast sounds a lot like a giant ground sloth. From what we know, they were huge red-haired animals. They were faster than the sloths we know today, which are very slow. Ground sloths had big claws that curled under and faced backward. It seems that they stood on their hind feet. They did this to eat the leaves and twigs in the trees above them.

What do you think? Should scientists search the Amazon for living giant ground sloths?

Write your answers on your paper.

1. The mysterious beast of the Amazon jungle is strong enough to
   a. break rocks
   b. tear apart a palm tree
   c. destroy large homes
   d. none of the above

2. True or false? Most scientists agree that the animal in the Amazon rain forest has to be a giant ground sloth.

3. In the fourth paragraph, the word *accompanied* means
   a. driven crazy
   b. frightened
   c. goes together

4. Describe a giant ground sloth in your own words.

5. True or false? Scientists believe the last of the giant ground sloths died more than 10,000 years ago.

6. What do you think is the most interesting characteristic of the legend of the Amazon rain forest?

7. Did giant ground sloths move faster or slower than today's sloths? How do you know?

8. What do scientists believe the giant ground sloths were doing when they stood on their hind feet?

Hey!
Why Not Write About It?

You don't have to be a famous player or even a supertalented one to have fun playing sports. Whether you enjoy being part of a traveling summer baseball team or just tossing a ball around in your backyard after school, it's important just to get out, exercise, and have some fun. Write about the kinds of sports and other outdoor activities you enjoy. Tell about one of your favorite sports memories.

Fold & Read: Nonfiction • ©The Mailbox® Books • TEC61376

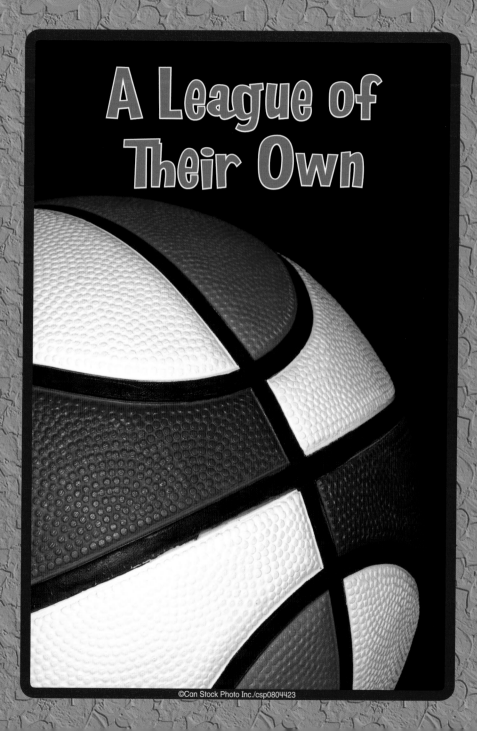

A League of Their Own

The Harlem Globetrotters basketball team members play in a league of their own. They are not part of the National Basketball Association (NBA) or any other league. But they are known all over the world. The players amaze their fans with their superb basketball skills. They also make their fans laugh with plenty of comedy routines during their games. The fact is that their play rivals even some of the best teams in the big leagues.

When the team of African American players first formed in 1926, it was because the young men just wanted a chance to play. At that time, black players could not join any pro team in the United States. So the Globetrotters had their pick of the best African American players in the country.

The team went through the Midwest to play games. They chose the name New York Harlem Globetrotters even though they were formed in Chicago, Illinois. Team owners thought the name would add mystery. Curious fans would then come out to see games with local teams. The Globetrotters were soon winning every game they played.

In the middle of a game in 1939, the Globetrotters were winning by a lot, 112 to 5. So team members began goofing around on the court. The crowd loved it. After that, the team's funny stunts became a part of each game if it had a strong lead. Soon that was the way they played from start to finish.

Some Harlem Globetrotters players have had great professional careers in the NBA. Still others, such as Meadowlark Lemon and Fred "Curly" Neal, became household names. And today, the Globetrotters truly do trot to places all over the globe. They bring their family-friendly act and high-flying basketball talent to cities both large and small.

Write your answers on your paper.

1. In what city were the Harlem Globetrotters originally formed?

2. Give the reason why these young African American basketball players first came together.

3. True or false? The Harlem Globetrotters are the funniest team in the National Basketball Association (NBA).

4. Harlem is a large neighborhood in New York City that has become famous over the years for its African American culture. Do you think the name Harlem Globetrotters is still a mysterious sounding name? Why?

5. In what year did the Globetrotters first begin goofing around on the court?

6. What does the term *household name* mean in the fifth paragraph?
  a. a name people were not allowed to say
  b. another name for a two-story house
  c. so well-known everyone knew who they were

7. In what region of the United States did the Globetrotters play their first games?
  a. Northeast   c. Southwest   e. none of these
  b. Southeast   d. Northwest

8. True or false? The Harlem Globetrotter players have never been good enough to play professional basketball in an organized basketball league.

Hey!

Why Not Write About It?

Imagine that you are an astronaut who is the first person to walk on the moon in over 50 years! What would you like to do and see while you are on our moon? What would your visit be like? Is there anything you would like to discover about the moon?

Fold & Read: Nonfiction • ©The Mailbox® Books • TEC61376

Earth's Natural Satellite

Our neighbor in outer space is the moon. It is much smaller than Earth. The distance across the moon is just over 2,000 miles. Right now, the moon is a little less than 240,000 miles away. Yet each year, the moon moves about 1½ inches away from Earth. Yes, the moon is *very* slowly leaving us, even as it circles fully around the Earth once every 29½ days.

While it appears quite bright in the night sky, the moon does not give off its own light. The light of the sun reflecting off the moon's surface is what makes it shine. From Earth, sometimes the moon does not look round. Sometimes we see no moon at all. But it's always there. It is the way the sun's light hits the moon that makes it look different. Also when we look at the moon, we always see the same parts. That's because the moon is spinning at just the right speed so that the same side is always facing us.

The first US astronauts landed on the moon in 1969. They went to learn about Earth's closest neighbor. While walking on the moon, they had to wear space suits. They also had to use oxygen stored in their backpacks to breathe. The astronauts left behind four mirrors. Scientists aim lasers at these mirrors to measure the distance between Earth and the moon.

Of course, other planets have moons too. According to NASA, the US space agency, there are at least 146 moons in our solar system. Mars has two moons. Neptune has 13, and Jupiter has 50, including the largest moon of all. The planet with the most moons is Saturn. It has 53.

Finally, did you know that the moon is why we have high and low ocean tides? The pull of the moon's gravity causes water to bulge toward the moon as it orbits Earth. Without the moon, we'd never have low tide at the beach!

Write your answers on your paper.

1. In what year did astronauts from the United States first land on the moon?

2. What is the approximate distance from Earth to the moon?

3. What is one thing astronauts did while they were exploring the moon?

4. True or false? Because of the speed at which the moon spins, here on Earth we always view the same parts of the moon.

5. Other planets in our solar system also have moons. Which planet has the most moons? Which planet has the largest moon?

6. True or false? Without the moon, high tide would be higher and low tide would be lower.

7. How did astronauts breathe while they walked around on the moon?

8. Does the moon have its own light? How do you know?

Hey!
Why Not Write About It?

When people think of squid, they might first think about the more common small squid and not the giant squid. Think of a common, small animal—such as a squirrel, dog, or gerbil—and then imagine what a giant version of it might be like. Describe your new giant animal—from what it looks like to what it eats to whether you and your classmates should be scared of it.

Fold & Read: Nonfiction • ©The Mailbox® Books • TEC61376

Mighty Mollusks: The Giant Squid

There is a family of over 100,000 undersea creatures known as mollusks. Members of this family include *gastropods*, such as snails and slugs; *bivalves*, such as clams, oysters, and mussels; and *cephalopods*, such as squid and octopuses. Some cephalopods use arms to catch their prey and then crush it with tough jaws. To think that there's a giant squid in the ocean that can grow to 60 feet is enough to make you think twice about your next trip to the beach!

People used to tell tales of giant sea monsters that crushed ships and attacked whales. Those tales may have been about giant squid. They're big, but they're not monsters! Sure, giant squid have eyes as big as a human head, but they use those eyes to see in the darkness deep in the ocean. Giant squid are believed to live in many parts of the world's oceans. They spend most of their time at depths of 1,000 to 3,300 feet.

Giant squid hunt other kinds of squid and fish, but they are also hunted! Sperm whales eat giant squid. Giant squid fight the whales to protect themselves, but they do not attack ships! They also don't attack whales themselves or attack people. In fact, it's very rare for a human to see a giant squid anywhere.

Most of what we know about giant squid comes from dead squid found washed up on beaches around the world or caught in fishing nets. Sometimes, scientists learn about giant squid by examining parts of the mollusk found in the stomachs of sperm whales. That's how we know they have eight arms, two longer tentacles, their large eyes, and a large beaklike mouth. Squid also have a tongue covered in teeth that shred the squid's prey when it is eaten.

There may be 100,000 different kinds of mollusks living in our oceans, but the giant squid is definitely the most impressive.

Write your answers on your paper.

1. What are three examples of bivalves?

2. How many different types of mollusks live in our world's oceans?

3. Which of these is an ocean depth in which you probably *won't* find giant squid?
   a. 3,000 feet deep
   b. 200 feet deep
   c. 1,700 feet deep
   d. none of the above

4. Which of these definitions best fits the use of the word *family* in the first paragraph?
   a. a basic social unit consisting of parents and their children
   b. a group descended from a common ancestor
   c. all the persons living together in one household
   d. a group of related things, as categorized by scientists

5. True or false? Giant squid often attack and destroy ships at sea.

6. Which of these is *not* a subset of mollusk?
   a. cephalopod
   b. gastropod
   c. escapod
   d. bivalve

7. List some of the distinguishing features of a giant squid that scientists have discovered when looking at dead specimens.

8. Why do you think it is rare for scientists to find examples of giant squid in the wild, whether living or dead?

Hey!
Why Not Write About It?

Think about all the ways in which we use written language. Now write about how your life would be different if all written forms of language disappeared.

Fold & Read: Nonfiction • ©The Mailbox® Books • TEC61376

Sequoyah Writes the Cherokee Language

Called "The Lame One" by his friends because of his weak legs, Sequoyah grew up in the mountains of present-day Tennessee. He was part of the Cherokee Indian tribe. Born around 1770, his father was a white soldier, trader, and explorer. Sequoyah's mother was a royal princess. His grandfather was a great chief. Though he grew up watching the other children play, it was Sequoyah who would become one of the greatest Cherokees of all.

Sequoyah was a quiet, shy boy. He spent much of his time in the woods drawing. He liked working with his hands and became a craftsman. Eventually, he became a silversmith. Sequoyah married and started a family. One day, white men came to his town with a treaty. The treaty gave the native tribe guns and blankets in exchange for land. Sequoyah was troubled. The chiefs agreed to the treaty. This was because the chiefs could not read the white men's words. In the end, the white men took more land than they had agreed to.

Sequoyah's people were learning English. He didn't like seeing them abandon their native language. So he stopped hunting and planting crops. Instead, he focused on one thing—writing Cherokee-language words on paper. He created a symbol for every syllable in the Cherokee language. At this time, Sequoyah's wife became very upset with him. He was ignoring his silversmith work! She threw all his written work into a fire. It was destroyed. What did Sequoyah do? He started over. He completed a written Cherokee language in 1821.

Sequoyah did something no one had ever done before by making up a written language all by himself. He was honored by his people and by the president of the United States. Sequoyah died in 1843. Yet the spirit of this small, weak-legged Cherokee man lives on. The tallest trees in the world, the sequoias, are named after him.

Write your answers on your paper.

1. How was Sequoyah different from the other Cherokee children?

2. Sequoyah's father was a white man. Which of these was *not* one of his trades?
   a. explorer
   b. horse trainer
   c. soldier
   d. trader

3. How did Sequoyah's wife destroy his written-language work?

4. Why was Sequoyah's physical handicap so much more of a challenge than it might be today? Think about how different life was for people in the late 1700s as compared to now.

5. Why did Sequoyah end up as one of the greatest Cherokees of all?

6. True or false? While creating the Cherokee written language, Sequoyah made his living as a shopkeeper.

7. Sequoyah was called "The Lame One" when he was a child. Explain what you think the word *lame* means in this context.

8. How do you think Sequoyah would react to learn that one of the largest and strongest trees in the world is named for him?

Hey!
Why Not Write About It?

Think of five words that are synonyms for the word *fast*. Use those words in five sentences about your own fictional encounter with mustangs in the wild. Did you manage to ride a mustang? Did the mustangs have special powers? Describe the sound of a band of horses running in the wild. Be creative!

Fold & Read: Nonfiction • ©The Mailbox® Books • TEC61376

Wild Mustangs

The word *mustang* might make you think of one of two fast things. It might make you think of a fast car racing down the track. You can hear its engine roar. Perhaps the word *mustang* makes you think of a fast, sleek fighter plane from World War II. You can imagine it swooping through the clouds. There was a time not so long ago when the word *mustang* meant the same thing to everyone; it meant a wild horse.

The first mustangs that ran across the western frontier were most likely horses that ran away from early Spanish explorers. The word *mustang* is thought to have come from the Spanish word *mestenos* or *mestengo*, meaning strayed, or ownerless horses.

Mustangs are small compared to most horses. They are only about 4½ feet high. This is probably because they do not eat as much as more common horses. The mustang's diet is a survival tool. Mustangs are wild and cannot count on daily feed from human beings. They learned to survive on what little food they could find. This is hard in harsh winters or very dry summers.

Mustangs have developed another important survival tactic. They live in groups called bands. Each band has a leader. The leader claims a grassy field for its family group. It looks out for the other horses in its band. When it feels the band is in danger, the leader makes sure the horses run away to stay safe.

Today, there is not much land left for these wild horses to roam. Experts think about 32,000 mustangs still gallop through ten western states. A small group of about 100 mustangs live in Assateague Island National Seashore off the coast of Maryland. Now when you hear the word *mustang*, you'll always think of a fast, wild horse!

Write your answers on your paper.

1. Which of these things is not known as a mustang?
   a. World War II airplane
   b. wild horse
   c. group of fast sailboats
   d. American-made sports car

2. Why do you think there are mustangs living on an island off the coast of Maryland when most other mustangs are found in the western states?

3. Describe one of the mustang's essential survival tools.

4. Where do people think wild mustangs come from?

5. True or false? Because they have had lots of room to roam outside of fenced pastures, mustangs are larger than more common horses.

6. Why might the leader of a band of mustangs suddenly make its entire group start running?

7. What qualities, or attributes, of the wild horse do you think designers thought of when developing the Mustang airplane and the Mustang car?

8. In your own words, what does the word *frontier* in the second paragraph mean?

Hey!
Why Not Write About It?

One of the difficulties scientists have when they study the sun is knowing just how hot it is. It's so hot, there's no way to send a space probe anywhere near it to get better pictures or samples of the gas ball's surface. Imagine you are the scientist in charge of building a probe to send to the sun. What would you design?

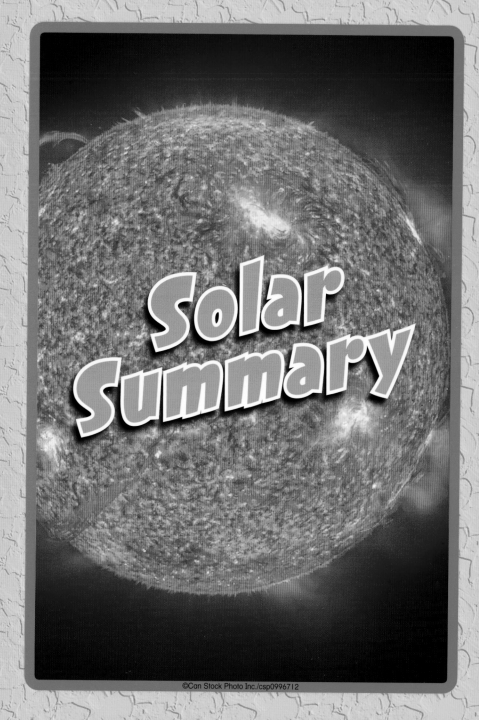

Solar Summary

W here would we be without our closest star? We'd be in the dark, that's where we would be! The sun is a big, hot star about 93 million miles from Earth. Its surface temperature is close to 10,000° Fahrenheit (F). The center of the sun is even hotter. It can reach over 27,000,000°F.

Scientists study the sun to learn all they can about this star that's been shining for more than four billion years. They think it could shine for another five billion years. Thanks to scientific studies, we know a lot about our closest star. The sun gives out light, heat, and other energy.

Hydrogen and helium are the two most plentiful elements that help make up the sun. These and other elements are fuel for the sun's process of nuclear fusion. Nuclear fusion reactions deep inside the sun produce the sun's energy. Yet the surface of the sun is not a simple place either. There are cooler areas called *sunspots*. There are also eruptions called *flares*.

The sun seems to rise with us in the morning and set with us at night. Of course, it's really the earth's rotation that causes night and day. The sun is always shining on the side of the earth that faces it. As Earth spins, light from the sun hits different sections. That means that it's always daytime somewhere on our planet. The sun never sets. We just tell ourselves that it does. The sun is not going anywhere anytime soon.

While the sun may appear to be small in the sky, it is more than 100 times larger than Earth. The distance across the surface of the sun is about 864,000 miles. How big is that? Well, if the sun were hollow, you could fit 1,000,000 earths inside it. And it would still be very hot.

Write your answers on your paper.

1. What is the temperature of the surface of the sun?

2. Because the sun never actually sets, do you think it would be possible to keep walking away from a sunset and toward the sunrise? Explain.

3. If you live for another three billion years, will the sun still be shining? How do you know?

4. True or false? There are patches of ice on the sun's surface called *sun rinks*.

5. How would you describe to someone the difference between the size of Earth and the size of the sun?

6. What do nuclear fusion reactions produce?

7. Which of the following is the way the sun turns its own fuel into heat, light, and other energy?
   a. nuclear fission
   b. nuclear inconsistency
   c. nuclear heavy water
   d. nuclear fusion

8. What are the two most common elements found in the sun?

◆◆◆◆◆◆

Hey!
Why Not Write About It?

For thousands of years, humans used parasites, such as leeches, to treat human medical conditions. Modern medical treatment saw that these practices stopped. Now researchers have found that using leeches to treat some problems may actually be a good idea. Would you allow a doctor to treat you with bloodsucking leeches? Why or why not?

Fold & Read: Nonfiction • ©The Mailbox® Books • TEC61376

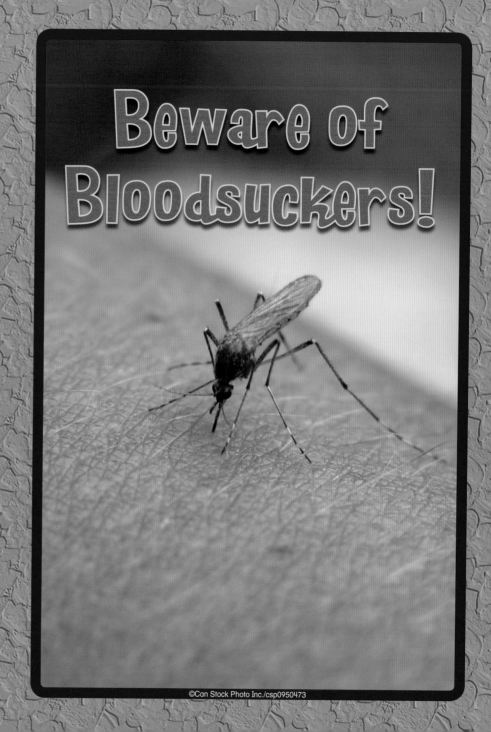

Beware of Bloodsuckers!

Bloodsuckers are all around us—in the air, on the ground, in the water. What are these pests? They are parasites. They feast on the blood of living creatures, though most of the time, they don't hurt their hosts.

At least 60 different kinds of leeches live in lakes and streams in the United States. These slimy worms have flat, narrow bodies. Some are shorter than half an inch while others are more than 20 inches. A leech attaches itself to a warm body. Then it uses its sharp mouthparts to saw into the skin and suck out blood. Still, leeches aren't all bad. They have been used by people to suck the poison out of snakebites. Their saliva may help prevent blood clots in humans and speed healing.

Another creature that feeds on blood is the louse. Known collectively as lice, they are wingless insects. They can live on mammals and birds. Their tiny pale bodies make them hard to see. They use the curved claws at the ends of their legs to cling to hair, feathers, or fur. Lice use their long, hollow beaks to suck up blood.

Ticks, another bloodsucking pest, hang out in fields, deserts, and woods waiting for animals or humans to pass by. A tick sticks out its front legs and then catches hold of a passerby with its claws. The tick burrows its head under its host's skin. Then it sucks blood and swells up like a balloon.

Not all bloodsuckers crawl or swim. The mosquito flies. It has two wings, six long legs, and a small body. The female has a long, hollow mouth that contains a sucking tube. The female mosquito finds a soft spot on a host's skin and begins feeding. She is done in about two minutes, but her bite has a chemical that keeps the host itching for much longer.

The next time you feel that itchy, creepy feeling, take a close look! You may have a bloodsucking pest along for the ride.

Write your answers on your paper.

1. Name the three environments in which ticks can be found.

2. What do we call the pests that feast on the blood of their hosts?
   a. lice
   b. parasites
   c. spam
   d. suckers

3. What are some tips this article gives readers for avoiding becoming hosts to parasites?

4. How many different kinds of leeches are found in the lakes and streams of the United States?

5. In what ways are leeches, ticks, lice, and mosquitoes similar? How are they different?

6. Which of the four types of bloodsucking pests is the hardest one to see?

7. True or false? All bloodsucking parasites are flightless.

8. What do you think are the best ways to keep yourself free of bloodsucking parasites?

Hey!

Why Not Write About It?

Imagine what it would be like to spend a day as a squirrel. Now write about it. Describe what your day is like from the time you wake up in the morning high in a tree until the time you go to sleep at night, again, high up in your treetop bedroom. What's it like living in the trees and coming down to the ground to look for a snack? Do you get chased by a dog?

Fold & Read: Nonfiction • ©The Mailbox® Books • TEC61376

Wild About Squirrels

Picture an animal with strong jaws. Picture the animal with sharp claws. Picture the animal with a parachute-like tail. Now imagine that this fantastic creature lives in forests, in cities, and in your own backyard! Does the thought of such an animal so close give you the heebie-jeebies? Relax. It's just a squirrel.

There are about 270 different species of squirrel. They are found on every continent except Australia and Antarctica. For most of us, when we hear the word *squirrel*, we think of one of the 122 types of bushy-tailed tree squirrels.

Tree squirrels have powerful jaws and four sharp front teeth. They use these features to gnaw through hard-shelled nuts and thick pinecones. Sharp claws and strong legs allow a squirrel to leap from tree to tree.

A squirrel's large tail has many uses too. It provides balance. It acts as a parachute to slow the animal if it falls and a cushion when it lands. A bushy tail is also a perfect blanket when it is cold. Plus, the tail acts as a rudder when the squirrel goes for a swim, helping steer it through the water. A squirrel also uses its tail to signal from a high perch to warn others to get away.

With their soft, furry bodies and bright eyes, squirrels may look tame. However, squirrels have a wild nature and can carry diseases that spread to people. So give a squirrel some space while you enjoy watching its unique behavior up in the trees or when it scampers quickly across the ground.

Write your answers on your paper.

1. What does a squirrel use its teeth and jaws for?

2. How many different species of squirrels are there?

3. A squirrel's teeth, claws, and tail seem like good things to have for living life in the trees. What other physical characteristics do you think would be good for a squirrel to have?

4. True or false? Bushy-tailed squirrels are only found in the forests of eastern Australia.

5. How does a squirrel use its tail in the water?

6. What characteristics of squirrels are enough to make people scared of one before they have even seen one?

7. In the first paragraph, a squirrel is called a "fantastic creature." Write your own definition of the word *fantastic* as it is used here.

8. Do you think a squirrel would make a good pet? Explain your answer.

Hey!

Why Not Write About It?

It is hard to imagine a time when mail was moved across the country by a few young men riding horses. Today much of our communication with people far away happens either on the phone, by text, or by email. Use your imagination to describe how we will talk to friends and family far away 20 years or 100 years from now.

Fold & Read: Nonfiction •©The Mailbox® Books • TEC61376

Heroes on Horseback

Would you risk your life to deliver the mail? Would you ride a series of horses at a full gallop across more than 75 miles of dangerous frontier land each day to deliver the mail? Would you consider several months to be a long time for mail to travel from New York City to San Francisco?

The brave young men of the pony express risked their lives to deliver the mail. By carrying it across a stretch of nearly 2,000 miles, the young riders cut the delivery time from weeks to around ten days. They rode fast horses for many hours at a time. Some rode through deserts. Other riders crossed flooded rivers. Some rode through mountains. Still others rode through wind, rain, and snow. All the while, they carried the mail.

The pony express was started in 1860 by a California senator and a Missouri businessman. They collected about 400 fast horses for the nearly 80 riders they hired. They set up 190 pony express stations across the route. None of the riders were over the age of 20. Most carried pistols and a knife. They had to watch for attacking Native Americans.

How did the pony express work? A rider left from one station with a mailbag and rode as fast as he could. After 10 or 15 miles, he arrived at the next station and traded for a fresh horse. Then he rode again. The rider's turn was up after he had covered about 75 miles. In this way, the mail moved day and night.

In the end, the pony express operated for about 18 months. It was put out of business by the transcontinental telegraph. During the time it operated, the express transported 34,753 pieces of mail, with the young riders covering more than 600,000 total miles.

Write your answers on your paper.

1. Describe some of the qualities you think a rider needed to work for the pony express.

2. How many miles would one pony express rider travel each day?

3. In your own words, tell what you think the word *frontier* means in the first paragraph.

4. Could a 19-year-old girl become a pony express rider in 1860? Why or why not?

5. Which of the following definitions best fits the word *transcontinental* in the last paragraph?
   a. around the world   c. across the country
   b. through the west   d. within Wyoming

6. Describe in your own words some of the dangers a pony express rider faced on a daily basis.

7. True or false? The pony express moved mail 24 hours a day.

8. Write the text evidence from the article that supports your answer to number 7.

Hey!
Why Not Write About It?

Soccer is a sport that has been around for many years. It is played throughout the world. What is your favorite sport? Is it difficult for just anyone to play? Why or why not? Write about your favorite sport, why you like to play it, and why you think other people should play it too.

Fold & Read: Nonfiction • ©The Mailbox® Books • TEC61376

Soccer Star

Soccer is one of the most popular sports in the world. It is played by millions of people. It is played in nearly every country. Big games are often watched on TV by billions of people. Why are people so crazy about soccer? It might be because people have been playing a version of soccer for over 2,000 years.

Rules for soccer, known in most countries as football, were set up in England in 1848. Since then, the current form of the game has spread to more than 200 countries. It is easy to play. It requires only a flat, open space and a ball. Men and women play. Boys and girls play.

Mia Hamm was one of America's first female soccer stars. At just 15 years old, she was asked to join the US National Team. She was the youngest player ever asked to join the country's soccer team. When Mia played on the 1996 US Olympic soccer team, fans really took notice of women's soccer for the first time. That year, the team won the gold medal. Reporters crowded around Mia to hear what the team heroine had to say. Mia spoke only of the team's effort.

To this day, Mia is the world's leading goal scorer in women's soccer competition. Her skill, sportsmanship, and sense of fair play helped her lead two teams to victory at the women's soccer World Cup in 1991 and 1999. She also led the 1996 and 2004 US Olympic team to victory. This made her a popular role model. She was soon one of the most famous women in all of sports.

Mia's example showed young girls it is okay to be tough. It's okay to compete. It's okay to want to win. Through the popularity of soccer, that message is carried to girls all over the world.

Write your answers on your paper.

1. Why do many people think Mia Hamm is a good role model?

2. List evidence from the text that supports this statement: Soccer is considered an easy sport to play.

3. In what years did Mia Hamm help lead the US soccer team to a World Cup victory?

4. The word *competition* in the fourth paragraph has several similar meanings. Which of the following definitions do you think fits best for how it is used in the article?
   a. rivalry to have more power than anyone else
   b. a contest for a prize or honor
   c. a competitor

5. In what country were the rules for soccer originally set up?

6. Why do you think the game of soccer has spread to so many other countries throughout the world?

7. True or false? Mia Hamm is well-known around the world.

8. List evidence from the text that supports your answer to number 7.

Hey!
Why Not Write About It?

In 1271, Marco Polo left Venice, Italy, for China. He was gone 24 years. When he returned, his home must have been much different. Imagine you are a space traveler. You have left Earth for an unknown destination. Where do you go? How long are you away? Describe what Earth is like when you return and what your reaction to the changes would be.

Fold & Read: Nonfiction • ©The Mailbox® Books • TEC61376

Marco Polo, Traveling Man

L'INDIE ORIENTALE,

In the year 1271, a 17-year-old named Marco Polo left his home in the port city of Venice, Italy. He went with his father and his uncle on their trade expedition to China. The Polos were merchants. Marco had been trained since he was young to understand foreign money, foreign products, and the handling of cargo ships.

The journey that began in 1271 was the second trip to China that Marco's father and uncle made. During their first trip, they had met Kublai Khan, China's ruler. He wanted to know all about Europe, Christianity, and the people of the West. He invited the Polos to return soon. So Marco joined his father and uncle. Together they set off on their long trip.

The travel was difficult. The caravan of merchants avoided raids by bandits. They crossed mountains. They survived deserts. It took them more than three years to reach the Khan's summer palace in China. There, Marco was amazed by the Khan's wealth. He befriended the ruler. The Khan liked that Marco knew four languages. He sent Marco on trips all over his kingdom. His travels lasted a long time. He learned about China's paper money, coal, postal system, and mining. After many more years, Marco, his father, and his uncle decided to go home.

The Polos returned to Venice. They had been gone 24 years. They brought back many riches, including ivory, jewels, and silk. Upon their return, the Polos found that Venice was at war. Marco was captured and put in jail. There he talked about his time in China. He told of the people he had met. He told stories of the amazing things he had seen. A fellow prisoner wrote down Marco Polo's story. It was called *Description of the World*. Marco was eventually freed and many people read his amazing story.

Write your answers on your paper.

1. When Marco Polo joined his father and uncle on their journey to China, was it the first time the older Polos went to see Kublai Khan? How do you know?

2. In your own words, describe what you think the word *befriended* in the third paragraph means.

3. How many years did it take Marco Polo, his father, and uncle to reach the Khan's summer palace?

4. In the third paragraph, what does the author mean by "caravan of merchants?"

5. Marco Polo, his father, and uncle were away from Venice for 24 years. What is the first thing you would do upon returning to your home after 24 years?

6. The Polo family made their living as merchants. Describe in your own words what you think a merchant is.

7. Name three items the Polos returned with from their visit to see Kublai Khan.

8. What things did Kublai Khan want to learn about from Marco Polo's father and uncle? Explain why you think the Khan was interested in these things.

Hey!
Why Not Write About It?

Dogs communicate in a variety of ways with each other, humans, and other animals. Most pets—whether they are cats, dogs, hamsters, or fish—look like they're trying to talk to us at one time or another. Think of your own favorite pet or animal. Write an imaginary conversation with that pet or animal about how your day has been so far.

Fold & Read: Nonfiction • ©The Mailbox® Books • TEC61376

Canine Conversation

Do dogs talk? What kind of question is that! Of course dogs talk. They don't use words like humans do. That's obvious. However, dogs communicate quite well with each other in a variety of ways. What's more, a dog owner can quickly learn basic dog-speak.

Dogs bark. That's one of their primary ways to communicate. A barking dog may be angry or making threats. However, a dog's bark often means it is alarmed about something. This type of message usually consists of two or three barks, followed by a pause, followed by another two or three barks. This could go on for quite some time. Yelling at a dog to stop its barking is actually telling the dog, "Yes, be alarmed! Keep barking." Experts suggest speaking to the dog in a calm voice. If the dog is your pet, give it a pat on the head. This tells the dog that everything is fine. It is time to stop barking.

Dogs also use body language. They wag their tails. In fact, they wag them in different ways depending on what they are trying to say. Dogs also move into different positions to send messages. For example, a dog that wants to play may lower its front end and stick its hindquarters and tail high in the air. The dog will look like it is bowing. Its face will be relaxed and its mouth slightly open. This is a dog's way of saying, "Let's play, pal!" On the other hand, what if a dog stands straight up with its ears and tail high, bares its teeth, and stares at you? Be careful. This dog may be angry. It may be protecting someone or something. It may be about to attack. Also, if a dog faces you with its ears flattened back, holding its tail low, and drawing back the corners of its mouth, watch out! This is a nervous dog that may attack out of fear. Stay away from a dog that does this.

Dogs use other means of communication too. This includes marking their territory with their scent; yelping, whining, and howling; and other behaviors. Watch a dog for a while, and you'll be able to figure out what it's telling you.

Write your answers on your paper.

1. Describe what a dog does to indicate that it wants to play.

2. What does the word *primary* mean in the second sentence of the second paragraph?

3. True or false? Barking is a dog's only method for communicating with people.

4. How do you know your answer to number 3 is correct?

5. If your dog is barking, is it a good idea to speak to it in a calm tone? Why or why not?

6. Describe other ways besides barking in which dogs communicate to each other and to humans.

7. Which of the following is the best definition of the word *yelping* in the last paragraph?
   a. to lick
   b. to utter a sharp, shrill cry
   c. to tumble backward
   d. to fall asleep

8. Why is a dog that is scared also a dog that might be dangerous?

Hey!
Why Not Write About It?

Imagine you are outside on a summer night when a spaceship lands in your backyard. Out of it comes a walking, talking Venus flytrap as tall as the tallest person you know. What does the flytrap want? Describe your encounter with the flytrap from outer space.

Fold & Read: Nonfiction • ©The Mailbox® Books • TEC61376

Venus Flytrap

Animals do many different things to survive. Some animals do a lot of different things to catch and eat other animals. While you wouldn't expect a plant to catch and kill an animal in order to survive, some do! Carnivorous plants exist all over the world. They're not mean. Nor can they run, hide, or hunt. They simply do what they need to do to live.

The Venus flytrap is a type of carnivorous plant. It is uniquely suited to catching and consuming the meat of unsuspecting insects. Each one of the flytrap's leaves ends in two lobes, or rounded parts. Each lobe has three stiff hairs on its surface and sharp spines around the edge.

When the sun shines and the weather is warm, the plant's trap is set. The red color of the lobes makes them look like a flower. The plant also has sweet nectar on its leaves. Insects can't stay away. So an insect flies close and lands on a lobe. It touches and bends the trigger hairs of the trap. Touching these hairs causes the lobes to snap shut. In half a second, the lobes close. The bug is caught, unable to get out. The spines on the edge of the lobes create a mini prison cell.

The lobes at the end of the plant's leaves continue to close until they are sealed. So is the fate of the insect! Once closed, the lobes secrete a liquid that digests the captured insect. The prey is digested within the leafy prison over the course of 12 days. When the meal is digested, the lobes open again. All you will see is the insect's hard outer shell that the Venus flytrap could not digest. The shell blows away in a breeze or is washed away by rain.

So insects beware! The flytrap never rests. It is always ready and waiting for its next meal.

Write your answers on your paper.

1. Write your definition of the word *carnivorous* in the first paragraph.

2. How does the Venus flytrap lure insects to it?

3. What do the trigger hairs on the flytrap's leaf lobes do?

4. True or false? It takes several minutes for a Venus flytrap's lobes to snap shut over an insect.

5. Tell how you know your answer to number 4 is correct. Use evidence from the text.

6. Describe the process by which the Venus flytrap digests its prey.

7. In the fourth paragraph, the word *secrete* means
   a. to form and give off
   b. to share special information
   c. to fold neatly
   d. to announce

8. Do you think it might be possible for an insect to survive being captured by a Venus flytrap? Why or why not?

Hey!

Why Not Write About It?

Pretend that you are a colonist who participated in the Boston Tea Party. What was it like to have Sam Adams speak to you about the importance of sending a message to the king of England? What was it like sneaking through Boston Harbor with hundreds of other colonists? Write a short account of your night at the Boston Tea Party, including the thrill and danger of doing something so important to our nation's birth.

Fold & Read: Nonfiction • ©The Mailbox® Books • TEC61376

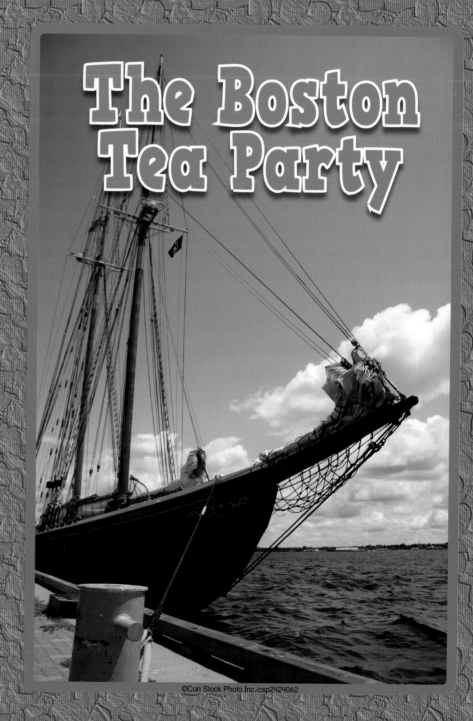

The Boston Tea Party

On the night of December 16, 1773, colonists living in Boston threw a party that is still remembered to this day. The party consisted of men dressed in old clothes. They put soot and red clay on their faces. The men tried to disguise themselves as Native Americans. The colonists carried hatchets, muskets, and clubs. They whooped and cried out as they headed into the dark night. Their destination? Boston Harbor.

You see, the colonists were mad about all the taxes they had to pay on goods that England sent to the colonies. This taxation had started in 1763. The British needed the tax money to pay for a war they had recently fought. The colonists boycotted the items that were taxed, buying other things instead. In 1773, the British put a tax on tea, which they knew people in the colonies liked to drink. Then they sent seven sailing ships full of tea to Boston, where it would be unloaded and sold.

Sam Adams, a leader of colonists in Boston, spoke to over 5,000 people at the Old South Meeting House. He and the people assembled agreed that the tea should be sent back to England. The colonists should not pay more taxes. Meanwhile, the British blocked the harbor so the ships full of tea could not leave.

That's when the colonists threw their tea party. Dressed as Native Americans, they went to the harbor. They boarded the ships, told the British officials to leave, and then went to work hacking open the crates full of tea. The contents of the crates were dumped into the harbor. Soon bags of tea bobbed across the harbor and the men slipped away into the night. "We have only been making a little saltwater tea," one participant joked.

This was just a first act in the rebellion that would eventually lead to the Revolutionary War. In this war, colonists would fight the British and gain independence for a new country, the United States of America.

Write your answers on your paper.

1. Why do you think the colonists dressed as Native Americans when they went to Boston Harbor to dump the tea?

2. In the second paragraph, what does the word *boycotted* mean?
   a. burned or destroyed
   b. took or stole
   c. refused to buy or refused to engage with

3. Why do you think the colonists were angry that the tax the British collected was spent on a war England had fought earlier?

4. Name the leader of the colonists who convinced a large gathering of Boston's citizens to join the tea party.

5. The British put a tax on tea because it was something people in the colonies would buy. What other product do you think they could have put a tax on that would have had the same effect?

6. Describe what the word *bobbed* means in the fourth paragraph.

7. How many British officials does the text say were hurt or killed on the ships the night of the Boston Tea Party?

8. What else do you think the colonists could have done to protest the taxes that England had placed on items being sold in the colonies?

Hey!
Why Not Write About It?

Pretend you are a journalist and get to interview a scientist who knows why mastodons disappeared from North America. Write your story and explain the scientist's theory.

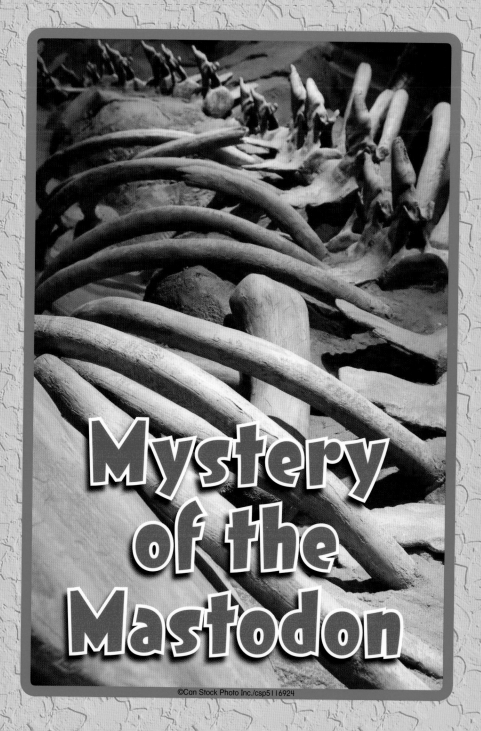

Mystery of the Mastodon

In its long history, our planet has been home to some amazing creatures. Many of these animals are now extinct, but we're unsure why. Besides the dinosaurs, there have been other enormous creatures that have roamed the land. Just think of the woolly mammoth, for example. The discovery of a mammoth's relative makes for an interesting true story.

In a marshy field on a farm in New York, ancient bones were hidden under the soil. By the time a farmer found them, some had crumbled to dust. Other bones had turned hard as stone, or fossilized. The bones were huge. No one knew what kind of creature these bones came from until Charles Willson Peale came along.

Peale, a famous portrait painter in the 1700s, started America's first natural history museum. Peale heard about the hip bones, tusk, and skull parts found on the farm in New York. He wondered if the bones were that of a mammoth. So he led a scientific trip to the farm. A five-foot-long piece of tusk the farmer found surprised Peale! Soon he hired local men and boys to begin excavating the soil. They found many more pieces of a huge skeleton, except a key piece. What Peale really needed was to find a jawbone. The summerlong digging went on until Peale found what he needed.

With the 60-pound jawbone in hand, Peale took the bones to his museum in Philadelphia. There he put the skeleton together. It was done after three months. A skeleton 15 feet long and 11 feet high stood before Peale when he and his aides finished. Although Peale called this creature a mammoth, a French scientist pointed out that it must be a mastodon. Mastodons had cone-shaped teeth, while mammoths had flat teeth. Peale's specimen had cone-shaped teeth. Still, why these huge animals vanished from North America is a mystery. Not even Peale could solve it.

Write your answers on your paper.

1. How do you think the farmer in New York began discovering bones on his land? What do you think he was doing at the time?

2. In the second paragraph, what does the word *fossilized* mean?
   a. to turn into a fossil
   b. to turn soft and brittle
   c. to become like gelatin
   d. none of the above

3. What was Charles Willson Peale famous for before putting together the mastodon skeleton?

4. Why do you think Peale was so surprised to find the farmer's five-foot-long tusk discovery?

5. Explain why a French scientist called Peale's mammoth skeleton a mastodon.

6. True or false? Peale's excavation at the farm in New York took place in the autumn.

7. Explain how you know your answer to number 6 is correct. Use evidence from the text.

8. Why do you think mastodons disappeared from North America?

Hey!
Why Not Write About It?

Imagine you are an astronomer who has been given the task of finding at least three new constellations in the night sky. What people, animals, and other objects do you find in the night sky? What do you name them? Explain why you choose the names you do.

Fold & Read: Nonfiction • ©The Mailbox® Books • TEC61376

Stars and Constellations

Did you know that the stars in the night sky do not have any points? We just draw them that way. Most stars are balls of gas that give off light and energy. Stars are formed when gravity pulls together dust and gas floating through the universe into spheres. The spheres grow smaller, and soon stars are born.

Groups of stars are called galaxies. The galaxy in which you find Earth is called the Milky Way. In the Milky Way, the star closest to Earth is our sun. The sun is so close that it does not just look bright—it also allows us to feel its heat. But our sun is just one of more than 100 billion stars in our galaxy. Depending on where you live, you may be able to see much of the Milky Way in the night sky. If you live close to a city or a very populated area, the many streetlights make it hard to see stars. People who live in areas far from large human populations can see many more stars in the night sky.

People living in ancient societies would look at the stars in the night sky and see forms and figures. In ancient times, of course, there were no streetlights. The stars in the sky were wondrous. These ancient people saw the outlines of humans, of warriors, of animals, and more. Today we call these shapes constellations. One easily seen constellation is called Orion. Orion was a handsome hunter in ancient Greek myths. Other, more common constellations are the Big Dipper and Little Dipper.

Stars can live for thousands or even billions of years. The light you see from stars at night is very old, having traveled for thousands of years to reach us. However, each star goes through a life cycle. Some start as clouds of gas, and many change into different types of stars before dying. Even our sun will one day fade into the final stage of a star and become a black dwarf. It makes you wonder: Is there someone on a faraway planet seeing our sun as just another star in the night sky?

Write your answers on your paper.

1. Explain in your own words why people who live in or near cities can see fewer stars in the night sky than people who live elsewhere.

2. The Milky Way is
   a. a star
   b. a beverage ancient Greek people drank at night
   c. the name of our galaxy
   d. both a and c

3. Define *galaxy*.

4. How long do scientists think most stars live?

5. What is the name given to the forms and figures people see in groups of stars in the night sky?

6. In your own words, explain how stars form.

7. What is a *black dwarf*?

8. True or false? According to this selection, Orion was an ancient Greek who named some of the most famous constellations.

Hey!
Why Not Write About It?

Now that you know more about the fish's behavior, could you jump into a South American river without thinking twice about piranhas? Describe the thoughts that might run through your mind as you swim in a river that might be home to piranhas.

Fold & Read: Nonfiction • ©The Mailbox® Books • TEC61376

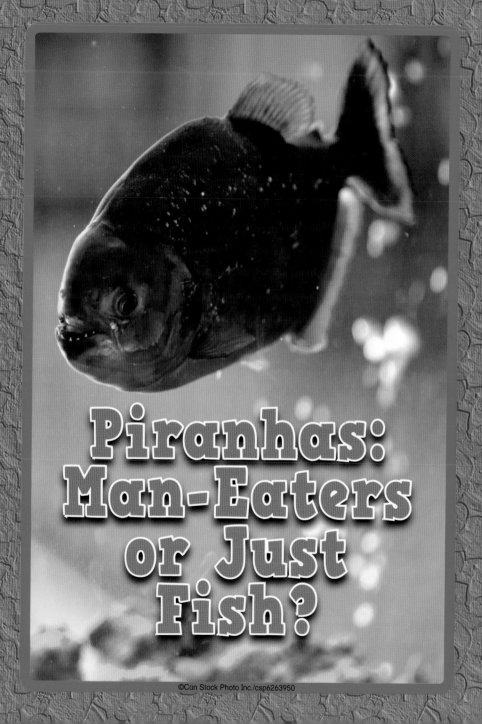

Piranhas: Man-Eaters or Just Fish?

If you got all your information from the movies, you would have some strange ideas about the world. You would think zombies are real, all sharks are man-eaters, and space travel is quick and easy. You also might think that piranhas are deadly eating machines that make a nice swim in a South American river a really bad idea. The movies, though, are not always accurate.

Piranhas live in lakes and rivers throughout much of South America's lowlands. They are a scary-looking fish. Piranhas do eat meat. However, they are not man-eating monsters. They do not swarm in huge schools to devour large animals. In fact, cases of piranhas attacking people are very rare.

There are dozens of species of piranhas. None grow much more than a foot long. All piranhas have sharp teeth that work like scissors. The fish takes small, bite-size chunks off its prey. That prey consists mostly of other small fish. Even then, most piranhas do not devour an entire fish. They usually take one bite of a fin or some scales or the tail. Piranhas also eat small birds, rodents, and frogs. When water levels are very high, a piranha might even eat seeds and fruit from submerged trees.

Piranhas are not fast swimmers, but they do know how to hunt. By hiding in plants or behind rocks, a piranha can sneak up on its prey. Some do hunt in groups, focusing on weak or sick fish in a school for their next meal. However, large schools of piranhas often form as a means of protection from the birds, larger fish, and river dolphins that want to eat *them*.

Sure, piranhas can look scary and be driven to attack any animal that enters its habitat when it is very hungry. But children in South America swim in the piranhas' waters all the time and are safe. So don't believe everything a movie tells you.

Write your answers on your paper.

1. Describe in your own words what a piranha looks like.

2. Name three things that piranhas like to eat, including one thing they find only during the wet season.

3. In your own words, define what the word *accurate* means at the end of the first paragraph.

4. True or false? Piranhas always travel in large groups, or schools, and swarm on their unsuspecting prey until nothing is left.

5. Tell how you know your answer to number 4 is correct. Use evidence from the text.

6. In your own words, define what the word *devour* means in the third paragraph.

7. Why do you think children in South America feel safe swimming in rivers and lakes where piranhas live?

8. Why, according to the author of this piece, should you not believe everything a movie tells you?

Hey!
Why Not Write About It?

May 25, 1935, was an amazing day in the life of young Jesse Owens. Although he would have an even more important impact on sports and history in 1936 at the Berlin Olympics, his record-setting day in 1935 was unforgettable. Can you think of another famous athlete or personality who has had an experience similar to Jesse Owens? Who is it? Compare your person to Jesse Owens.

Fold & Read: Nonfiction • ©The Mailbox® Books • TEC61376

Jesse Owens: The Buckeye Bullet

Ohio State University's athletic teams are nicknamed Buckeyes for the state's buckeye trees. Track-and-field legend Jesse Owens attended Ohio State University after a sensational high school track career, earning him the nickname the Buckeye Bullet. At the 1935 Big Ten track-and-field championship, Jesse set three world records and tied another. It was only his second year at Ohio State, but sophomore Jesse Owens put on "the greatest one-man athletic show in history," according to the newspaper the *Cleveland News*.

It was May 25, 1935, and Jesse turned up at the meet with a hurt back. The Buckeyes' track-and-field coach, Larry Snyder, thought Jesse might make his back worse if he competed. Yet Jesse begged Snyder to let him run. The two agreed that Jesse could run the 100-yard dash, but only if he took it easy.

The Buckeye Bullet dug his feet into the cinder track and waited for the starter's signal. When it sounded, Jesse bolted down the track and finished in just 9.4 seconds. Not only did he win the race, he tied the world record doing so. From there, Jesse headed to the long-jump pit for his next event. He wasn't thinking about his sore back. Less than ten minutes after tying the 100-yard dash world record, Jesse took his first and only long jump of the day. He jumped 26 feet, 8¼ inches! It was a new world record!

Jesse had two more events to run that day. In the 220-yard dash, he finished in just 20.3 seconds. He set another world record! Later, he ran the 220-yard low hurdles race. This run included jumping ten 30-inch-high hurdles. Jesse Owens finished in 22.6 seconds. No one before had done it in less than 23 seconds. Yes, the Buckeye Bullet set another world record, within 45 minutes after the 100-yard dash. The following year, Jesse made history at the 1936 Olympic Games in Berlin, Germany, winning four gold medals.

Write your answers on your paper.

1. Where does the nickname Buckeyes come from?

2. Explain in your own words why Jesse Owens was called the Buckeye Bullet.

3. What physical problem could have kept Jesse from competing at the Big Ten championship?

4. What does the word *sophomore* mean in the first paragraph?

5. How many world records did Jesse set on May 25, 1935?

6. The word *meet* in the second paragraph means
   a. to encounter someone for the first time
   b. dinner
   c. a gathering for competition

7. The equipment (including running shoes) and training that track-and-field athletes use has changed a great deal since Jesse Owens set his records. If Jesse was a college student today, do you think he would be considered a fast runner? Explain your answer.

8. What do you think the word *bolted* means in the third paragraph?

Hey!
Why Not Write About It?

Many scientists like David Johnston willingly put themselves into dangerous situations to study the things that interest them. Do you think you could be a scientist like him? Is it important for scientists to sometimes risk their lives to gain knowledge? Explain your answer.

Fold & Read: Nonfiction • ©The Mailbox® Books • TEC61376

The Loud Voice of Mount St. Helens

When you look at a mountain, you probably don't think it has a voice. You probably don't think of it as a living thing either. In 1980, two men in Washington State thought a mountain was speaking to them and, clearly, that it was also alive. One of those men was 83-year-old Harry Truman. He lived beside Mount St. Helens for years and operated the Mount St. Helens Lodge. Harry loved to talk to and about the mountain.

On March 20, 1980, a small earthquake rumbled across the remote region where Mount St. Helens is located. Seven days later, ash shot skyward and large cracks opened on the mountain's north side. As a result, the US Forest Service set up a command center in Vancouver, Washington, to monitor the mountain. Scientist David Johnston arrived to study what was happening. He could hear the voice of the mountain. David studied volcanoes. He knew this mountain was alive and its voice was growing louder.

On Saturday, May 17, David noted a huge bulge growing on the mountain's north side. The next morning, David observed the bulge and reported his latest readings to the command center in Vancouver. At 8:32 AM, David's excited voice crackled over the radio one more time. "Vancouver! Vancouver! This is it!" he shouted. Then the signal went dead. Why? Because the bulge that David had been watching suddenly burst with the power of a hydrogen bomb. Hot ash shot 60,000 feet into the air. Trees toppled. David, along with his trailer, jeep, and tools, vanished forever. So, too, did Harry Truman and his lodge. It was buried beneath 300 feet of mud and debris.

In the end, Mount St. Helens's voice was a loud and angry one. The mountain came alive. When the dust and ash finally settled, scientists found that the mountain was 1,300 feet shorter than before. And a 156-square-mile area northwest of the mountain had been leveled by the blast. It looked like the surface of the moon.

Write your answers on your paper.

1. In what year did the eruption at Mount St. Helens take place?

2. Why was Harry Truman in the area when the mountain erupted?

3. What does the word *toppled* mean in the third paragraph?

4. In your own words, explain why the area northwest of the mountain ended up looking "like the surface of the moon."

5. What does the word *vanished* mean in the third paragraph?

6. How do you think David Johnston felt when he sent his last message? Give evidence from the text to support your answer.

7. Why do you think the US Forest Service wanted to monitor Mount St. Helens?

8. How were Harry Truman and David Johnston alike? How were they different?

Hey!
Why Not Write About It?

There are raft spiders, which are like fishermen. There are trap-door spiders, which spring out from behind a trapdoor to catch their prey. Now play the part of a scientist who has discovered a new kind of spider. What do you name this newly discovered spider, and why do you pick this name? Explain the spider's behavior and what it is about this spider that made you think this was a good name.

Fold & Read: Nonfiction • ©The Mailbox® Books • TEC61376

Spiders: Fearsome or Fascinating?

Eight legs. Sharp fangs. Poison glands. Sticky silk from its spinnerets. Two, four, six, or even eight eyes. These are all attributes of spiders. How you react to the very thought of a spider gives you an idea of how most people think of spiders. They're nightmarish, fearsome creatures creeping up on you in the night!

Well, no, they really aren't. In fact, spiders are much more fascinating than they are fearsome. It may not comfort you to know there are more than 30,000 different kinds of spiders. Some are smaller than the head of a pin, while others are the size of a dinner plate. Some disguise themselves in order to catch their prey. For example, there's the bird-dropping spider, which—yes—looks like bird droppings. There's also the ogre-faced stick spider, which looks like a thorn or a twig. Creepy? Absolutely. Fascinating? You bet!

Want to be creeped out even more? Then meet the raft spider, which eats small fish and tadpoles. Like a fisherman, it lures its prey to the water's surface and then dips its head in the water to take a bite out of a passing tadpole. The trap-door spider lives in a tunnel and builds a door over it. When an insect passes by, the trap-door spider rushes out to grab its prey.

While most spiders do carry poison, few are able to harm humans. In the United States, we must watch out for black widow and brown recluse spiders. Their bites are painful but can be treated by doctors. However, one of the most dangerous of all spiders is the Brazilian wandering spider of South America. It has been found in bananas shipped to North America. These spiders are bad news, so stay away from it if you find one among your grocery store bananas!

Still, most spiders are harmless. They have more reason to be afraid of us than we do of them. Besides, spiders eat lots of insects. And insects are pretty creepy too!

Write your answers on your paper.

1. What does the author of this passage imply about how most people feel about spiders?

2. What does the word *attributes* in the first paragraph mean?
   a. body parts
   b. problems
   c. characteristics
   d. methods

3. A spider's silk comes out of its body through spinnerets. Is *spinnerets* an appropriate word to describe this spider body part? Why or why not?

4. How is a raft spider like a fisherman?

5. There are two types of venomous spiders in the United States. Do you think that is enough reason to fear *all* the spiders you see? Why or why not?

6. In your own words, tell what the word *lures* means in the third paragraph.

7. The word *fearsome* means
   a. scary
   b. dangerous
   c. awkward
   d. contagious

8. Does the author think spiders are fearsome or fascinating? How do you know?

Hey!
Why Not Write About It?

Here's your big chance! Many people have ideas for a book they'd like to write, whether it is for kids, adults, or both. If you could write a book for your friends, family, and teachers to read, what would it be about? Give it a title and explain why it would be a fun book to read.

Before They Were Our Favorites

Three popular writers, whose books you surely know, took unexpected journeys to success. They may not have set out to become best-selling children's authors, but that's where they ended up.

If one of your favorite all-time books is *Green Eggs and Ham* by Dr. Seuss, you must know good writing. If your dad was a school principal, your mom was a nurse, and you were a school teacher for ten years, you must know a thing or two about what kids like and that they learn a lot when they're having fun! Combine all that with a love for myths, legends, fairy tales, and humorous books, and you might be ready to write books for young people. That's what Jon Scieszka (pronounced *SHES-ka*) did. The author of the Time Warp Trio series and *The True Story of the 3 Little Pigs!* started out as a teacher and became a best-selling author.

Lots of kids like to doodle. Many draw cartoons. Most do not go on to become best-selling authors. However, Jeff Kinney did. Jeff drew cartoons for his college newspaper; then he went on to use his video gaming and computer skills for websites like funbrain.com and poptropica.com, which he created. While doing this work, Jeff started writing and drawing a book about his experiences in school. Nine years later *Diary of a Wimpy Kid* was published. It quickly became a bestseller.

J. K. Rowling wrote her first book when she was six. It was called *Rabbit*. Knowing that being a writer was all she ever wanted, J. K. Rowling kept track of stories and memories from her school years. On a train trip as an adult, these memories of school and her friends turned into a story about a young boy named Harry who goes to wizard school. During much of the writing of the first Harry Potter book, J. K. Rowling didn't have a job or much money to support herself and her daughter. Today, thanks to Harry Potter, J. K. Rowling is one of the richest people in the world!

Write your answers on your paper.

1. What did authors Jeff Kinney and J. K. Rowling both base their stories and characters on?

2. What did Jeff Kinney do with his cartooning skills during college? What did he do for work after leaving college?

3. What does the word *doodle* mean in the third paragraph?

4. In your own words, describe what the term *best-selling author* means.

5. What is one of author Jon Scieszka's favorite books of all time?

6. Choose one of the three writers in the passage. Name a word that describes the writer. Provide evidence from the text to support your choice.

7. Why do you think it took nine years between the time Jeff Kinney started writing and drawing *Diary of a Wimpy Kid* to get it published?

8. List three things you learned from this article about how to become a successful writer.

Hey!
Why Not Write About It?

Write a news story that describes the discovery of a saber-toothed cat living near you. How is it caught? How has it survived? What is done with this living piece of history?

The Saber-Toothed Cat and Today's Tigers

The next time you look at your pet cat or a friend's pet cat, imagine it a little bigger. Not the ten pounds the average house cat weighs. Imagine it weighing nearly 750 pounds. Imagine if it were about five feet long! Add to that a set of canine teeth the shape of sabers, or swords, over eight inches long. Now you have a basic idea what the saber-toothed cat might have looked like.

Saber-toothed cat

Long known as the saber-toothed tiger, the animal described above became extinct more than 10,000 years ago. It wasn't really a tiger at all. Scientists can only guess what it looked like. They think this large cat had spotted fur. Its coat may have looked like that of a jaguar or cheetah. This would have kept it camouflaged. Its tail was short, which meant it had worse balance than most types of cats do.

Like the modern tiger, the saber-toothed cat was a fierce and scary predator. At 750 pounds, it was nearly all muscle. With its long, saber-shaped teeth and short, strong legs, the saber-toothed cat hunted large prehistoric creatures such as mastodons and giant ground sloths. It probably needed its long teeth to tear through the thick skin of its prey.

Saber-toothed cat fossils have been found in Europe, Africa, and North and South America. Today's tigers, the largest member of the cat family, are found only in Asia. Some live in the tropical jungles of Thailand. Some are found in the hot, dry thorn woods of India. Still others are found in the cold, snowy spruce forests of Siberia. Tigers are generally night hunters. They stalk deer, antelope, wild cattle, and wild pigs. Unlike lions, tigers prefer to be in shade and do not hunt on open plains. If the tiger is a relative of the extinct saber-toothed cat, it may tell us something about how the prehistoric cat lived and hunted.

Write your answers on your paper.

1. Name three of the four continents where saber-toothed cat fossils have been found.

2. Why do you think saber-toothed cat fossils have *not* been found on the other three continents?

3. Choose the best definition for the word *extinct* in the second paragraph.
   a. moved elsewhere
   b. to die out
   c. live underground
   d. was sick

4. Describe in your own words the size of a fully grown saber-toothed cat.

5. How did the saber-toothed cat get its name?

6. On what continent are tigers found?

7. True or false? Tigers live only in tropical jungles.

8. How do you know your answer to number 7 is correct? Use evidence from the text.

Hey!
Why Not Write About It?

Would you make a trip to see the Marfa lights or the Hornet Ghost Light? Why or why not?

Fold & Read: Nonfiction • ©The Mailbox® Books • TEC61376

Spooky Lights

Unexplained lights in the night sky may give you the heebie-jeebies! People see strange lights in the sky all over the world. Is it lightning? No. These lights seem to shine, glow, burn, and even hum or buzz. People try to find reasons to explain away the lights. However, many such mysteries remain unsolved.

Ghost lights are one kind of unexplained light that people have seen. One ghost light is famous enough to have once had its own museum called the Spook Light Museum near Joplin, Missouri. Here, locals told of a light in the night sky they had dubbed the Hornet Ghost Light. It has been seen by many people over the past 100 years. One legend tells that this is light from a lantern held by a missing miner. Pretty spooky, don't you think?

Near the desert town of Marfa, Texas, ghost lights are seen so often by local residents and visitors that the state has created an official viewing site. In the 1880s, a young settler saw the lights. He thought they were the campfires of an Apache tribe. When people searched for the ashes of the campfires, they found nothing. No one had camped where the lights were seen. Over the years, many people have tried to explain the Marfa lights. Yet they remain a mystery to this day.

Scientists and others have tried to explain the Marfa and Joplin ghost lights. One common idea is that they are the reflections from car headlights. Many people do not agree. While no evidence exists, first reports of these lights come from a time before cars or even roads. Other spooky lights are thought to be burning methane gas. The methane comes from decaying plants. These lights are often seen near marshy, wet areas. But Marfa and Joplin are in drier environments. So what causes the ghost lights? Not knowing is enough to send shivers down your spine!

Write your answers on your paper.

1. True or false? Some people think that these mysterious lights are the result of hydrogen explosions in the atmosphere.

2. How do you know your answer to number 1 is correct?

3. The word *dubbed* in the second paragraph means what?
   a. uncovered
   b. to be painted
   c. given the name
   d. buried beneath a rock

4. Do you think the Marfa, Texas, ghost lights are the result of methane gas burning? Why or why not?

5. When did settlers first report lights in the night sky of Marfa, Texas?

6. Is the Spook Light Museum still open? How do you know?

7. In your own words, describe what a legend is based upon the word's use in the second paragraph.

8. What do you think the Hornet Ghost Light really is?

Hey!
Why Not Write About It?

You are zipping through the Milky Way galaxy in your brand-new alien spacecraft when, suddenly, there's a problem with your engine. You need to land your ship on the nearest planet to see what's wrong. When you land, strange creatures gather around to see who and what you are. You look at your maps and realize you are on the planet called Earth. Describe what your first 30 minutes on Earth are like.

Is Anybody Out There?

©Can Stock Photo Inc./csp1722528

The residents of Woking, England, thought the object in the night sky was a shooting star. It left a glowing, green streak behind it. When residents found the crash site the next morning, there was a large crater. In it, an object was covered in soft sand. News spread quickly and many onlookers came to see it. This was no meteorite, but some sort of metal tube. It stilled glowed, hot from its descent through the atmosphere to Earth. It made strange sounds. As people watched it began to open. Eyewitnesses expected a man to emerge. Instead, two enormous black eyes peered out of the opening and then a mass of tentacles! An oily, brown creature as big as a bear emerged. People scattered in every direction. They feared for their lives.

That alien encounter, from *The War of the Worlds* by H. G. Wells, was written in 1898. Yet people have reported seeing "fiery dragons" and "flying ships" in skies around the world for hundreds of years. Today we call them UFOs, or unidentified flying objects. In 1947, some people started calling them flying saucers after an American pilot said that nine circular objects that looked like saucers were flying near his plane.

People who study UFOs are called ufologists. During the 1950s and '60s, official United States Air Force ufologists studied more than 12,000 UFO sightings. This was called Project Blue Book, an official government investigation. Of the 12,000 reports, only 701 could not be explained.

No one knows for sure if we live on the only planet with intelligent life or if we are being visited by alien beings. There are billions of stars in space. Some may have planets that can support life. SETI, the Search for Extraterrestrial Intelligence, listens for radio messages and other signals from outer space. SETI astronomers have sent their own messages into space in case someone or something out there is listening. In the meantime, we keep our eyes turned to the night sky.

Write your answers on your paper.

1. Explain what a ufologist does.

2. Why do you think so many people came to look at the object that crashed in the setting of H. G. Wells's story?

3. How did flying saucers get their name?

4. Project Blue Book was
   a. a high school play about UFOs
   b. a book by H. G. Wells
   c. SETI's original constitution
   d. a US Air Force investigation

5. In your own words, describe what an eyewitness is.

6. True or false? People have only been seeing UFOs for the last 75 years.

7. How do you know your answer to number 6 is correct? Use evidence from the text.

8. Do you think UFOs are real? Explain your answer.

Hey!
Why Not Write About It?

Think about a toy or object that you have had for as long as you can remember. If it was going to have something to do with a grown-up career, what might the career be? Would you like this job? Why or why not?

Fold & Read: Nonfiction • ©The Mailbox® Books • TEC61376

Jane Goodall and the Chimpanzees

Most children get nice presents when they are two years old. Have many of the toys you got on a birthday turned into your life's work? That's what happened to Jane Goodall. Jane was born in England in 1934. For her second birthday, her parents gave her a stuffed toy chimpanzee. It didn't frighten her as some relatives suspected it would. Instead, she was fascinated. As Jane got a little older, she spent much of her childhood watching animals. In fact, she once spent five hours inside a stuffy henhouse waiting to see a hen lay an egg. Why? Because she wanted to know how it happened. By the time she was eight, Jane told her mother that one day she wanted to go to Africa to live with animals.

Jane was determined. When she was old enough, she went to work as a secretary at a documentary film company. In her spare time, she studied all she could about Africa and its animal life. She went to the Natural History Museum. And she took a second job to earn money to save for a trip of a lifetime. Finally, at age 23, she had saved enough!

Jane traveled to Kenya, a country on Africa's east coast. She met Dr. Louis Leakey, a well-known scientist, who gave her a job digging up fossils. But Jane wanted to study *living* animals. Dr. Leakey got her another job. She went to Gombe National Park in Tanzania to study chimpanzees in the wild. It was difficult. The chimps feared her. Soon they got used to her, and she could get closer and closer. One of her discoveries about chimpanzees was that they made and used tools. This was incredible!

Two years later, Jane returned to England. She attended Cambridge University and earned a doctorate degree in animal behavior. Then she returned to Tanzania and started the Gombe Stream Research Center. Her study of the area's chimpanzees continues to this day. Her articles and books have appeared around the world, and Jane has become a face of the wildlife conservation movement—all because of that first stuffed toy chimpanzee present.

Write your answers on your paper.

1. Where was Jane Goodall born?

2. What two events in Jane Goodall's early life were sure signs that she wanted to study animals when she was a grown-up?

3. In your own words, describe what the word *determined* means in the second paragraph.

4. Who helped Jane get her start in Africa?

5. What was an important discovery that Jane Goodall made about chimpanzee behavior?

6. Do you think it was important for Jane Goodall to eventually return to England and Cambridge University to earn her doctorate degree in animal behavior? Why or why not?

7. Describe in your own words what you think the wildlife conservation movement is.

8. What do you think Jane Goodall's relatives would say about her stuffed toy chimpanzee today?

Hey!

Why Not Write About It?

Pretend it is the 1890s. You are the same age as you are now, and you witness one of the first automobile races. Describe in a letter to a friend your feelings about seeing these huge, hard-to-control cars careening as they raced down your dusty farm road. Keep in mind that the first racecars were not very fast and very few people had even seen a car before.

START YOUR ENGINES!

As long as there have been automobiles, there has been automobile racing. The sport began in the 1890s. Of course, those races were a lot different than the ones we see on television today. Those first races were on winding, hilly dirt roads that were made by horses and wagons. There was nothing special about the cars that raced. If you could afford to buy one, you could race it. The cars were hard to drive. They had weak brakes and were hard to steer. Not only that, people who came to watch didn't think about safety. They stood at the edge of the road. If a driver lost control, fans could be hurt or killed.

The first big changes in car racing came after World War I. During the war, engineers made smaller and stronger engines. This meant racecars could be smaller too. And they were faster. People like speed. Race fans wanted to see cars going faster. The sport became more popular, and people started paying to see races. However, rules were different at each race. This made it hard for drivers to compete.

In 1947, after another war resulted in even more engine improvements, a mechanic and driver named Bill France held a meeting with other racecar drivers in Daytona Beach, Florida. Tired of the different rules for every race, Bill helped form a group that would have the same rules for every one of its races. The group was called NASCAR for the National Association of Stock Car Auto Racing. In 1949, the group held its first race. It was on a dirt track in Charlotte, North Carolina. The following year, the first NASCAR paved track opened in Darlington, South Carolina.

Television allowed people all over the country to see automobile races. A race fan in California could watch a live broadcast of a race in Florida. Interest in racing continued to grow. However, it was NASCAR that fans loved the most. Today it is one of the most popular sports in America.

Write your answers on your paper.

1. Why was the sport of automobile racing dangerous in the 1890s?

2. Describe what the word *afford* means in the first paragraph.

3. What historic event changed early automobile racing?

4. What advances made in two wars helped the sport of auto racing?

5. In your own words, describe what the word *winding* means in the first paragraph.

6. Why did Bill France bring racecar drivers together in 1947?

7. What organization resulted from the meeting Bill France held in Daytona Beach, Florida, in 1947?

8. What do you think is the biggest change in automobile races since the 1890s? Give reasons for your answer.

Hey!
Why Not Write About It?

The story of *Titanic* has been told in several movies and in many books. We know quite a bit about the disaster from survivors. Now it's the iceberg's turn. Tell the story of the dramatic sinking of *Titanic* from the iceberg's point of view.

Fold & Read: Nonfiction • ©The Mailbox® Books • TEC61376

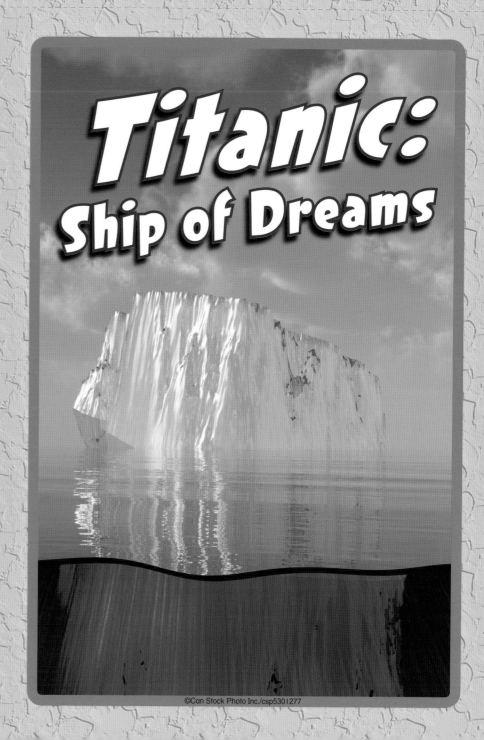

Titanic:
Ship of Dreams

There are a lot of numbers to remember when you read about the R.M.S. *Titanic*. At the time of its first voyage, *Titanic* was the world's largest and most luxurious ocean liner. At 882½ feet, the ship was almost as long as three football fields. From the bottom of its keel to the top of its funnels, the ship measured 175 feet—as tall as an 11-story building. Those dimensions are certainly big. Yet the tragedy of *Titanic* is even bigger.

Titanic sank on the night of April 14, 1912. It was 400 miles southeast of Newfoundland. At around 11:40 that night, while cruising at top speed through calm waters, the ship sideswiped a mountain of floating ice. It scraped hard against the iceberg below the waterline. Seawater flooded in. The ship was made of 16 watertight compartments. It could remain afloat if two of those were flooded. However, five quickly filled with cold seawater.

Many of the ship's 2,207 passengers and crew were asleep when the accident occurred. That there were only enough lifeboats for 1,178 people made the disaster go from bad to worse. An orchestra played on the ship's deck as passengers were put into the lifeboats. The music was meant to keep people calm. Many were afraid to leave *Titanic* and thought it safer to remain aboard the "unsinkable" ship. One lifeboat meant to hold 65 people was rowed away from the sinking liner with only 19 passengers. Two-and-a-half hours after striking the iceberg, *Titanic* made a thundering groan. Then it split into two sections and sank into the ocean, carrying 1,517 people to their deaths.

Hours later, a ship called *Carpathia* arrived. The people in the lifeboats were rescued. More than 70 years later, a team of scientists found the remains of *Titanic* nearly 12,500 feet down in the Atlantic. They retrieved the warning bell from the ship's crow's nest, along with dinner plates, personal items, and other artifacts. But the huge vessel will forever remain under the sea.

Write your answers on your paper.

1. What does the word *dimensions* mean in the first paragraph?
   - a. definitions
   - b. measurements
   - c. descriptions
   - d. questions

2. Did rough seas play any part in the ship's sinking? How do you know?

3. True or false? All of *Titanic*'s lifeboats were filled with many more passengers than they were designed to hold.

4. How do you know that your answer to number 3 is correct? Use evidence from the text.

5. What is the best meaning for the word *retrieved* in the last paragraph?
   - a. destroyed
   - b. cleaned
   - c. got back
   - d. lost

6. Describe what the word *sideswiped* means in the second paragraph.

7. What is one thing that might have prevented the *Titanic* tragedy?

8. If you could find out anything more about the fate of *Titanic* and her passengers, what else would you want to know? How would you go about getting answers?

Hey!
Why Not Write About It?

Several different popular books and movies have told the fictional stories of modern-day scientists and explorers who found living dinosaurs walking the earth. Imagine you have stumbled upon living dinosaurs while on vacation with relatives. Write a letter back to your teacher telling him or her all about your discovery.

Fold & Read: Nonfiction • ©The Mailbox® Books • TEC61376

Dinosaurs:
They're Not All Extinct

By the time you're old enough to read, you're old enough to understand that dinosaurs became extinct about 65 million years ago. Meat eaters and plant eaters alike suddenly died out. You can go to a museum or a national park and see dinosaur fossils. But you can't go to a zoo and see a living dinosaur. Or can you?

Go fishing in the Indian Ocean with the right bait and you might just land yourself a dinosaur. That's what happened to some fishermen in 1938. They caught a pale pink and blue fish with silver markings. It was five feet long and unusual looking. They took the fish to a woman who ran a museum. She determined the fish was a coelacanth (pronounced *SEE-luh-kanth*). Scientists thought these fish had died out 80 million years earlier. Yet they are still caught today!

Perhaps you've heard of the Komodo dragon (see this booklet's cover). Not really a dragon, it is the largest living lizard. Komodo dragons are meat eaters with jagged teeth and sharp claws. They live on islands in Southeast Asia. While some people claim they can grow as big as 30 feet long, the largest one scientists ever measured was ten feet long. Still pretty big for a meat-eating lizard and a lot like a meat-eating dinosaur!

Then there's the tuatara. It's a lizard that lives on small islands off the coast of New Zealand. It's a three-eyed lizard with a bony arch on its head. This arch links it to a family of dinosaurs that became extinct 60 million years ago. Tuataras can live for up to 80 years. The female lays eggs that take up to a year or more to develop. And that third eye? It helps the tuatara judge the time of day and the season. This cold-blooded reptile, unlike other reptiles, can stay active in cooler temperatures.

When you look at a coelacanth, a Komodo dragon, or a tuatara, you're looking at more than just a living fossil. You could say you're looking at a modern-day dinosaur!

Write your answers on your paper.

1. How many years ago do most scientists think dinosaurs became extinct?

2. In what ocean would you have your best chances of catching a fish that dates back to the era of the dinosaurs?

3. Describe what the word *determined* means in the second paragraph.

4. What distinctive body feature links the tuatara to its dinosaur ancestors?

5. Explain why you think some people say the Komodo dragon can grow up to 30 feet long when scientists have only measured them as long as ten feet.

6. True or false? The tuatara is a cold-blooded reptile that can hunt only in warm temperatures.

7. How do you know that your answer to number 6 is correct? Use evidence from the text.

8. Which of the three animals in the text do you find most interesting? Why?

Hey!
Why Not Write About It?

Pretend that Teddy Roosevelt is going to be a guest speaker in your classroom. First, list five facts you want Teddy to know about life in your classroom today. Then write five things you want to know about Teddy Roosevelt. Use complete sentences in both lists.

Booklet 33

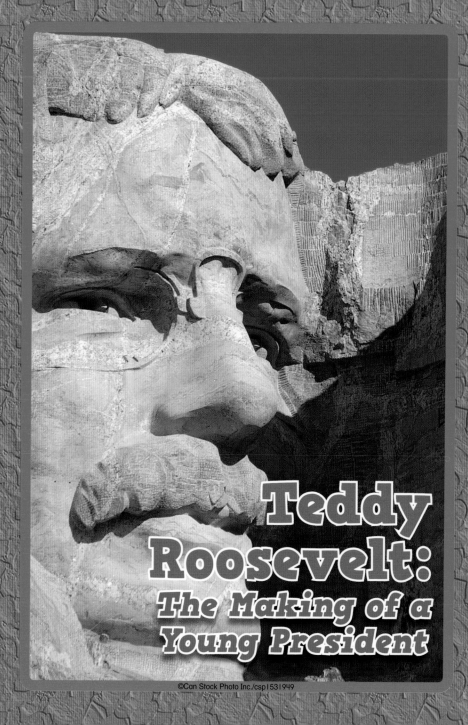

Teddy Roosevelt:
The Making of a Young President

Theodore Roosevelt Jr. was born on October 27, 1858. He was a sickly child who grew into a man people called a cyclone. Known as Teddy, the future president suffered from asthma as a child. He was often sick. He couldn't go to school. So Teddy was tutored at home. He loved reading and studying the outdoors. He didn't let his asthma slow him down. Teddy traveled to foreign lands with his family. The young man made himself strong in a gym his parents built for him in their house.

Teddy also became an excellent student. In 1876, he started college at prestigious Harvard University. Teddy met his wife Alice at Harvard. After graduating from college, Teddy returned to New York and decided to go into politics. Other politicians admired his courage, intelligence, and enthusiasm. Sadly, Teddy's mother and Alice died on the same day in 1884. A grief-stricken Teddy left New York. He went to the Dakota Territory and took care of his cattle ranches.

In 1886, Teddy returned to New York and married his childhood friend Edith. They started a new life. Teddy would have five children with Edith in addition to his daughter he had with Alice. Teddy's reputation had grown tremendously by the time he recruited cowboy soldiers for the Spanish-American War. This group was known as the Rough Riders. Teddy became a hero in the war. Shortly after, Teddy was elected governor of New York.

In 1900, Teddy was elected vice president of the United States. Not long after taking office, the president died and Teddy became president at the age of 43. Later, he was elected to a second term. His enthusiasm, courage, and intelligence never waned. He won the Nobel Peace Prize for helping end a war between Japan and Russia. He supported the building of the Panama Canal. And he established many national parks. Teddy died in 1919 at the age of 61. He is one of the four presidents whose face is carved on Mount Rushmore.

Write your answers on your paper.

1. Although Teddy Roosevelt suffered from asthma as a child and couldn't go to school, he grew to be a strong and very outgoing man. What did his family do to make sure Teddy overcame the challenges from his childhood?

2. Describe what the phrase "*slow him down*" means in the first paragraph.

3. True or false? In 1900, Teddy Roosevelt was elected by the American people to be the president.

4. How do you know your answer to number 3 is correct? Use evidence from the text.

5. Where did Teddy Roosevelt meet his first wife?

6. Explain what you think *grief-stricken* means in the second paragraph.

7. The text describes Teddy Roosevelt as courageous. List one piece of evidence from the text that supports this description.

8. What is the best meaning for *waned* in the last paragraph?
   a. became less
   b. increased
   c. made sense
   d. was confusing

Hey!
Why Not Write About It?

In this booklet's reading selection, you read about unusual objects, such as fish and pennies, falling from the sky. Write a short story about a time when you witnessed something strange falling from the sky.

Fold & Read: Nonfiction • ©The Mailbox® Books • TEC61376

Weird Weather

Raindrops and snowflakes falling from the sky? Yes. Fish and maggots? Yuck, no thanks! For centuries, there have been reports from just about every part of the world of strange things raining down from the sky. What explains such weird weather?

Fish and frogs would seem to top the list of things that fall from the sky other than raindrops and snowflakes. Flounder fell on London streets in 1984. That same year, sea stars fell in North Yorkshire, England. A century earlier, bean-size frogs rained on the town of Derby. In 1859, a woodworker in Wales was starting his work when he felt something fall on his head. Unsure what it was, he put his hand down the neck of his shirt and pulled out a handful of small fish. They dripped their way out of the sky!

Other parts of the world have seen their share of weird weather in the last 150 years too. How would you like to be rained on by slimy snails? That happened to residents in parts of Pennsylvania in 1869. Frogs covered Kansas City in 1873. Snakes slithered out of the sky onto Memphis in 1876. Sardines fell in Australia in 1989. In 1968, maggots rained down on a boat race in Mexico! Double *yuck*!

Weird weather isn't just about animals falling from the sky. In 1956, it rained pennies in parts of England. Thirty years later, more than 300 apples rained down on the yard of an English couple. Elsewhere, people have reported chunks of ice, nails, bricks, and even flowers raining down from the sky.

What causes this weird weather? Scientists and experts have been guessing and investigating such strangeness for hundreds of years. Still the best answer seems to be that winds that form tornadoes and waterspouts pick up these things and cause them to rain down from the sky miles and miles away. So grab your umbrella and watch out!

Write your answers on your paper.

1. What is the best meaning for the word *residents* in the third paragraph?
   a. people who work outside
   b. visitors
   c. people who live permanently in a place
   d. scientists

2. What fell from the sky first in England?

3. Describe what the word *weird* means as it is used in the title of this selection.

4. True or false? Weird weather like the events described in this selection have happened only in the last 150 years.

5. How do you know that your answer to number 4 is correct? Use evidence from the text.

6. According to the selection, what did people witness falling from the sky in 1876?

7. Are scientists sure that they have an explanation for why these things and animals fall from the sky? How do you know?

8. What would be another good title for this selection?

Hey!
Why Not Write About It?

Congratulations! You have invented a satellite designed to clean up space junk that is orbiting Earth. Astronauts, scientists, and others are very excited about your idea. In fact, they want you to come to a special celebration to thank you for your hard work. Write a short thank-you speech. Make sure to mention how your satellite will work.

Fold & Read: Nonfiction • ©The Mailbox® Books • TEC61376

Space Junk

Space is a very big place. Yet rocket and satellite launches, as well as routine space missions, result in lots of debris. The debris is a ring of space junk around our planet. Scientists currently track over 10,000 pieces of junk that measure more than four inches. They do this using very powerful radar and telescopes.

Why keep track of space junk? Imagine what happens when a bolt or other piece of space junk hits a satellite traveling more than 17,000 miles per hour! That's going to do some damage. Scientists want to make sure the very expensive satellites and spacecraft they send into orbit will be safe. They do that by staying aware of large pieces of space junk.

Space junk may include nuts, bolts, paint chips, camera lens caps, and tools. Very large debris includes satellites that don't work anymore and rocket boosters and their parts from satellite launches. Some space junk is just that—junk. Sometimes a new satellite collides with an old satellite. The result? Lots more junk!

Small pieces of space junk, called silver bullets, are much harder to track. While they are hard to see, they can still do lots of damage. Remember, space junk is moving pretty fast. Silver bullets can dent satellites and spacecraft. And think of the danger to astronauts working outside a space station! Scientists estimate there are more than 400,000 silver bullets shooting through space.

So what do we do about space junk? Astronauts try not to make more of it. Scientists keep track of it. A lot of the junk eventually falls back to Earth and burns up in the atmosphere. Some experts have suggested building garbage truck satellites—robots that orbit the planet and pick up the junk. Until that happens, we'll have to live with junk floating around our planet and try not to create additional debris.

Write your answers on your paper.

1. Write the two synonyms (words with similar meanings) in the first paragraph.

2. Why is it so important for scientists and space agencies to keep track of space junk?

3. What term is used to describe very small pieces of space junk?

4. What happens to a lot of the space junk in Earth's orbit?

5. Which of the following definitions is best for the word *debris* in the first paragraph?
    a. sadness
    b. uncertainty
    c. broken-down remains
    d. paper

6. What is one idea scientists have for cleaning up space junk?

7. Give three reasons why you think there is so much space junk orbiting our planet.

8. What would be a good name for a robot that collects space junk?

Hey!

Why Not Write About It?

How exciting do you think life gets in a typical day for a jellyfish? Write today's date on a sheet of paper and write a diary entry for yourself as if you were a jellyfish. What was your day like, drifting quietly through the ocean?

Fold & Read: Nonfiction • ©The Mailbox® Books • TEC61376

Not Really a Fish

Drifting through the water carried on ocean currents sounds like a peaceful way to live. For the most part, jellyfish are peaceful creatures. Like most animals, they need to eat to survive. They also have their fair share of enemies. Also, like land animals, some types of jellyfish are quite dangerous. Most of all, jellyfish are fascinating creatures that are best observed from a safe distance.

Jellyfish are invertebrates (they have no backbones) that have been around for millions of years. Although they look like blobs of jelly, they do have muscles. These muscles allow them to contract their bell-shaped bodies to push out water and propel themselves through the ocean. Still, they are not strong enough to swim far or fast. That's why they mostly just drift along.

When you look at a jellyfish—some of which can grow to 7 feet across—you don't see eyes, ears, teeth, or a brain. However, they do have sensors. These sensors allow them to smell, taste, and determine light from dark. They have a type of mouth inside their body (or bell). They also have four to eight oral arms around their mouth and tentacles that hang down from the edges of the body. These arms and tentacles capture food. Most jellyfish stun or kill their prey with their tentacles. Jellyfish like to eat plankton, tiny plants and animals that float in the ocean. They also eat fish and sometimes even other jellyfish!

To humans, most jellyfish stings cause just a mild irritation or burning. The sting of a few types of jellyfish, though, can kill a man within five minutes. Even the deadliest of jellyfish may find itself becoming someone or something else's snack. Ocean sunfish, leatherback sea turtles, other jellyfish, and even some people think jellyfish taste great! So while it may seem like drifting through life on an ocean current sounds nice, you may want to ask a jellyfish how much it likes it. But keep your distance!

Write your answers on your paper.

1. In your own words, explain what an invertebrate is.

2. True or false? Most jellyfish are good swimmers.

3. How do you know your answer to number 2 is correct? Use evidence from the text.

4. What is the largest some jellyfish can grow to?

5. What does the word *irritation* mean in the fourth paragraph?

6. Describe how a jellyfish is able to propel itself through the water.

7. Why did the author suggest observing jellyfish from a distance?

8. What would be another good title for this selection?

Booklet 1

Answers for 6 and 7 will vary.
1. b
2. false
3. camouflage and mimicry
4. the cane toad
5. c
8. It can flee from danger by running on water.

Booklet 2

1. c
2. off the coast of Cape Cod
3. false
4. b
5. treasure hunters; July, 1984
6. One of the survivors said there were 180 bags of silver and gold on the ship.
7. museums around the country
8. Answers will vary.

Booklet 3

Answers to 6 and 8 will vary.
1. Larry Page and Sergey Brin,1996
2. a
3. Answers should include three of the following: offers email service, hosts videos, provides an image search, provides directions, and makes software that runs smartphones.
4. c
5. false
7. true

Booklet 4

Answers for 4 and 6 will vary.
1. b
2. false
3. c
5. true
7. faster. We know this from what scientists have been able to determine.
8. Scientists believe giant ground sloths were eating leaves and twigs in the trees above them.

Booklet 5

1. Chicago, Illinois
2. They were not allowed to play on a professional level.
3. false
4. Answers will vary.
5. 1939
6. c
7. e
8. false

Booklet 11

1. fields, deserts, woods
2. b
3. The article does not give tips for avoiding parasites.
4. at least 60
5. They are similar in that they suck blood and have mouthparts that help them to do so. They are different in that mosquitoes can fly, leeches are found in lakes and streams and have some benefits for people, and mosquitoes also leave the host itching.
6. louse
7. false
8. Answers will vary.

Booklet 12

Answers for 3 and 8 will vary.
1. to gnaw through hard-shelled nuts and pinecones
2. about 270
4. false
5. as a rudder to steer
6. strong jaw, sharp claws, big tail
7. based on fantasy, not real

Booklet 13

1. Answers will vary but might include the following: good horse rider, brave, less than 20 years old, male, courageous, not afraid to use a pistol or knife, tireless, strong, small, and light
2. about 75 miles
3. *Frontier* in this context means a large, untamed expanse of land without many people in it. It is an area that has not been explored by many people.
4. Only males were hired.
5. c
6. attacks by Native Americans, rough weather, injuries, getting lost
7. true
8. "In this way, the mail moved day and night."

Booklet 14

Answers for 1 and 6 will vary.
2. "It is easy to play. It requires only a flat, open space and a ball."
3. 1991, 1999
4. b
5. England
7. true
8. "This made her a popular role model." "She was soon one of the most famous women in all of sports."

Booklet 15

1. no; The text says it was the second trip Marco's father and uncle had made.
2. to be a friend to
3. more than three years
4. group or party of merchants or travelers; the Polos and their guides
5. Answers will vary.
6. someone who buys, transports, and sells goods
7. Answers should include three of the following: ivory, silk, jewels, and riches.
8. Europe, Christianity, and the people of the West. Answers will vary.

Booklet 16

1. It may lower its front end and stick its hindquarters and tail high in the air. Its face will be relaxed, and its mouth will be slightly open.
2. first in order or importance
3. false
4. The text states that dogs also use body language and other ways of communicating.
5. yes; Yelling at a dog to stop barking is actually telling the dog to be alarmed.
6. body language; yelping, whining, and howling; marking their territory
7. b
8. Answers will vary.

Booklet 17

1. meat eating
2. Leaf-end lobes are colored to look like a flower. It has sweet nectar on its leaves.
3. cause the lobes to shut on an insect that has touched them
4. false
5. "In half a second the lobes close."
6. Once closed, the lobes secrete a liquid that digests the captured insect. The prey is digested over the course of 12 days.
7. a
8. Answers will vary.

Booklet 18

Answers for 1, 3, 5, and 8 will vary.
2. c
4. Sam Adams
6. floated on the surface
7. none

Booklet 19

Answers for 1, 4, and 8 will vary.
2. a
3. painting portraits
5. The teeth on the skeleton of Peale's creature were cone-shaped (like a mastodon) and not flat like those of a mammoth.
6. false
7. In the third paragraph, the text describes the digging as "summerlong."

Booklet 6

1. 1969
2. a little less than 240,000 miles
3. Astronauts put mirrors on the moon so scientists could use lasers to measure its distance from Earth.
4. true
5. Saturn has the most moons. Jupiter has the largest moon.
6. false
7. Astronauts carried oxygen in their backpacks.
8. no; The moon reflects light from the sun.

Booklet 7

1. clams, oysters, and mussels
2. more than 100,000
3. b
4. d
5. false
6. c
7. eight arms, two longer tentacles, large eyes, beaklike mouth, tongue covered in teeth
8. Answers will vary.

Booklet 8

Answers for 4, 5, 7, and 8 will vary.
1. Sequoyah was lame. He spent much of his time in the woods drawing.
2. b
3. She threw it into a fire.
6. false

Booklet 9

Answers for 2, 7, and 8 will vary.
1. c
3. They do not eat as much as common horses and eat more native, wild plants; or they live in bands, with a leader responsible for guiding the herd away from danger.
4. Mustangs of the western states are believed to have come from horses that ran away from early Spanish explorers.
5. false
6. to avoid danger

Booklet 10

1. about 10,000° F
2. Answers will vary.
3. yes; Scientists think the sun will still be shining as it is now for another five billion years.
4. false
5. If you could hollow out the sun, you could fit 1,000,000 earths inside it.
6. energy
7. d
8. hydrogen and helium

Answer Key Cards

Booklet 20
1. Answers will vary.
2. c
3. a group of stars
4. thousands to even billions of years
5. constellations
6. Gravity pulls together dust and gas into spheres. The spheres get smaller and become stars.
7. the name given to a star in one of its last life stages
8. false

Booklet 21
Answers for 1, 7, and 8 will vary.
2. small fish, small birds, rodents, frogs; In the wet season, they will also eat seeds and fruit from submerged trees.
3. free from error, precise, exact, correct
4. false
5. The text states that piranhas do not swarm in large groups to devour prey and that large schools form as a means of protection from predators.
6. to swallow or consume hungrily

Booklet 22
Answers for 2 and 7 will vary.
1. the Ohio buckeye tree
3. a sore back
4. a second-year college student
5. three
6. c
8. to start suddenly and quickly

Booklet 23
Answers for 4, 6, and 7 will vary.
1. 1980
2. He operated a lodge at the base of Mount St. Helens, a place where he had lived for many years.
3. knocked down forcibly
5. to disappear without a trace
8. Both men thought Mt. St. Helens was speaking to them and that it was alive. Both were on the mountain when it erupted, and both were killed. Truman stayed on the mountain because he didn't want to leave his home; Johnston was on the mountain to study the eruption.

Booklet 24
Answers for 3 and 5 will vary.
1. The author implies that most people have a fear of spiders.
2. c
4. It lures its prey to the water surface.
6. to attract or draw toward
7. a
8. fascinating; In the second paragraph, the author says spiders are more fascinating than fearsome.

Booklet 29
Answers for 6 and 8 will vary.
1. England
2. She received a stuffed toy chimpanzee when she was two that fascinated her. She later spent five hours in a stuffy henhouse watching a hen lay an egg.
3. displaying resolve to do something; making a firm decision and sticking with it
4. Dr. Louis Leakey
5. their ability to make and use their own tools
7. a worldwide collection of people and groups dedicated to preserving wildlife and the natural world

Booklet 30
1. Cars had weak brakes and were hard to steer. People who lined the sides of winding, hilly roads where races took place could get hurt if a car went out of control.
2. able to bear the cost of something
3. World War 1
4. Engineers made smaller and stronger engines.
5. full of turns
6. to establish a single set of rules for car races
7. NASCAR
8. Answers will vary.

Booklet 31
1. b
2. no; According to the selection, the ship was cruising through calm waters.
3. false
4. One lifeboat was rowed away with 19 passengers instead of the 65 that it could hold.
5. c
6. to strike with a blow along the side
7, 8. Answers will vary.

Booklet 32
Answers for 5 and 8 will vary.
1. about 65 million years ago
2. the Indian Ocean
3. decided
4. the bony arch on its head
6. false
7. The text states that the tuatara can stay active in cooler temperatures.

Booklet 33

1. Teddy Roosevelt's family had him tutored at home. They took him on trips to foreign lands. They built a gym in their home for him to use to build his strength.
2. He didn't let his asthma stop him from living an active life.
3. false
4. The text states that Teddy was elected as the vice president.
5. Harvard University
6. felt intense sadness
7. Answers will vary.
8. a

Booklet 34

1. c
2. frogs
3. unusual, unexpected, or out of the ordinary
4. false
5. The text states that there have been reports of strange weather for centuries. Also, the dates of events mentioned in the article span more than 100 years, and the last paragraph states that investigations have been conducted for hundreds of years.
6. snakes
7. no; The text states that scientists and experts have been guessing and investigating for hundreds of years, and that their explanation is the best answer.
8. Answers will vary.

Booklet 35

1. junk, debris
2. The debris can be dangerous to astronauts, space vehicles, and satellites.
3. silver bullets
4. A lot of the space junk in Earth's orbit eventually falls back to Earth and burns up in the atmosphere.
5. c
6. creating garbage truck satellites that would collect space debris as they circle the planet

7, 8. Answers will vary.

Booklet 36

1. a creature without a backbone
2. false
3. The text states that jellyfish aren't strong enough to swim far or fast.
4. 7 feet across
5. inflammation, soreness, or sensitivity on a body part
6. They contract their bodies to push out water, which causes them to move through the water.
7. Their sting can cause irritation or burning, and some jellyfish can be dangerous to humans.
8. Answers will vary.

Booklet 25

Answers for 6–8 will vary.
1. their experiences growing up
2. Jeff Kinney drew a daily cartoon for his college newspaper. After leaving college, he worked on websites.
3. to draw or scribble aimlessly
4. one whose book or books are listed on best seller lists
5. *Green Eggs and Ham* by Dr. Seuss

Booklet 26

1. Europe, Africa, North America, South America
2. Answers will vary.
3. b
4. It weighed about 750 pounds and measured about five feet long.
5. It is a member of the large cat family and had long canine teeth shaped like sabers.
6. Asia
7. false
8. The text states that tigers live in tropical jungles; in hot, dry thorn woods; and in cold, snowy forests.

Booklet 27

Answers for 4 and 8 will vary.
1. false
2. The text says that some people think the lights are reflections of car headlights or are the result of burning methane gas from decaying plants.
3. c
5. in the 1880s
6. no; The text states that the museum was near Joplin, Missouri, which implies it is no longer there.
7. a story that attempts to explain the start of something

Booklet 28

Answers for 2 and 8 will vary.
1. studies UFOs and the claims people make about witnessing them
3. In 1947, a pilot referred to nine circular objects near his plane that he described as flying saucers.
4. d
5. someone who experiences an event firsthand and can tell others what he or she saw
6. false
7. The text states that people have reported seeing UFOs for thousands of years.

Everyone's Talking About The MAILBOX® Books!

"When I buy books from The Mailbox® Books, I am confident that they will be useful. So far, I've never been disappointed."

Sandy Groom
Jacksonville, FL

"I absolutely love The Mailbox® books. Each book does an excellent job of matching the curriculum."

Kristie Jones
Van Wert, OH

"I can always depend upon The Mailbox® books to help make my job easier!"

Connie Neises
Emporia, KS

"I LOVE THEM! Every time I am searching for a skill or project, I know I can go through a book from The Mailbox® Books and find exactly what I am looking for!"

Gina A. Goble
North Brunswick, NJ

"I believe in The Mailbox® books because they provide age-appropriate ideas that blossom into lifelong learning!"

Linda Nance
Anaheim, CA

THE MAILBOX
The Education Center®

TEC61376

grades 4–6

Fold & Read NONFICTION

No-prep practice with reading informational text? It's yours in *Fold & Read: Nonfiction!* Inside each of the **36** already-laminated booklets, you'll find an engaging nonfiction text passage and questions that cover Common Core and state standards skills. Optional bonus activities and complete answer keys are also included. The booklets are perfect for independent practice, centers, small groups, or early finishers!

Bonus writing activity

Hey! Why Not Write About It?

When people think of squid, they might first think about the more common small squid and not the giant squid. Think of a dog, or gerbil—such as a squirrel, giant version of it might be like. Describe your new giant animal—from what it looks like to what it eats to whether you and your classmates should be scared of it.

Booklet 7

Nonfiction text passage

Write your answers on your paper.

1. What are three examples of bivalves?

2. How many different types of mollusks live in our world's oceans?

3. Which of these is an ocean depth in which you probably won't find giant squid?
   a. 3,000 feet deep
   b. 200 feet deep
   c. 1,700 feet deep
   d. none of the above

4. Which of these definitions best fits the use of the word *family* in the first paragraph?
   a. a basic social unit consisting of parents and their children
   b. a group descended from a common ancestor
   c. all the persons living together in one household
   d. a group of related things, as categorized by scientists

5. True or false? Giant squid often attack and destroy ships at sea.

6. Which of these is not a subset of mollusks?
   a. cephalopod   c. escargot
   b. gastropod   d. bivalve

Comprehension and vocabulary questions

Just tear out, fold, and use!

Mighty Mollusks: The Giant Squid

Engaging cover

Purchase Other Great Titles From The MAILBOX® BOOKS:

TEC61227.   Choose & Do Language Arts Grids • Grades 4–6
TEC61229.   Choose & Do Math Grids • Grades 4–6
TEC61374.   Fold & Solve: Math • Grades 4–6
TEC61398.   Warm Up, Practice, Test: Language Arts • Grades 4–6
TEC61401.   Warm Up, Practice, Test: Math • Grades 4–6

www.themailbox.com

ISBN

BORDEN'S
$ 17.95

9 781612 762555